Seneca and Elizabethan Tragedy

.

SENECA AND
ELIZABETHAN TRAGEDY

TO

MY MOTHER

CONTENTS

CHAP.   PAGE

  I THE DRAMA BEFORE SENECA .   .   I

 II SENECA THE MAN   25

III THE TRAGEDIES OF SENECA .   .   53

IV DARKNESS AND DAWN .   .   .   78

 V SENECA IN THE ELIZABETHANS .   110

    INDEX   135

PREFATORY NOTE

So short a work hardly needs preface or preamble. I wish only to express my indebtedness to Mr J. T. Sheppard for his reading and invaluable criticism of the proofs, and my hope that the book may be both of some definite use to students of the Drama and of some general interest to a wider circle of readers—in the Roman phrase of Lucilius—"neque indoctissimis neque doctissimis."

F. L. L.

KING'S COLLEGE, CAMBRIDGE.
18 *November* 1921.

CHAPTER I

THE DRAMA BEFORE SENECA

IN the realm of letters it has been Seneca's destiny, like Banquo's, to beget in his posterity a greatness denied himself. Virgil, that imperial poet, was the founder of a line of degenerate literary *fainéants*, the Epic poetasters of Silver Latin: but from Seneca, decadent Silver Latinist himself, by a seeming freak of fortune can be traced the direct descent of the lordliest names in the dramatic literature of Western Europe. To estimate his influence and to trace the line of descent from him to the Elizabethans is the main purpose of this book. But for the sake of completeness I have prefaced a slight sketch of the rise of the Greek drama, which made him possible, and of the Roman which led up to him, before dealing with Seneca the man, that strange compound of strength and weakness, brilliance and imbecility, and Seneca the writer, so second-rate, decadent and vulgar, yet with an ingenuity like Ovid's, almost genius, and an influence on Renaissance literature which really is amazing.

But before going into details it may be well to try to give the keynote of the whole, the thread that may be recognised running through even the earlier, but far more the later, part of our period of 500 B.C. to 1640 A.D. I mean that endless conflict which under a hundred different names is waged through all cultures, in all times and lands.

On the one side stands Classicism, in its widest sense, the feeling for the value of tradition, of form; for perfect form is of its nature the outcome of a long traditional evolution. And Classical minds and Classical periods are really only those in which are particularly realised the value of restraint, of law, of self-control, of construction in works of art, of an exact and perfect fitness in the relation of what the artist expresses to the frame in which it is expressed. Think of a Greek pediment, its elaborate symmetry, its adjustment of its balanced grouping to the sloping gable sides—an attempt only fully successful after centuries of effort and experiment and readjustment. Classicism is always conscious of the importance of "due measure"; it tends to care a great deal for faultlessness and flawlessness, a little too much, very often; to be intellectual rather than emotional and intuitive; it values rule, distrusts instinct; it criticises itself while it creates; it is produced not in a frenzy of inspiration, a "first fine careless rapture," but with labour and pain; its creations smell not of the wine-cup, but the lamp.

Such is one of the two combatants in the eternal duel, which may perhaps be called the battle of Classic and Romantic, always being fought, never decisively won. It is a conflict like the conflict of summer and winter; the happiest periods are those when neither is completely dominant.

So much then for Classicism: that is what I shall mean when I use the word. One needs to be a little careful and remember that many Greek and some Roman Classics are not in that sense strictly classical. Aeschylus is hardly to be roped in: but Sophocles is an example of such 'Classicism' at its best, and for 'Classicism' not at its best one may think of the orator Isocrates who spent nine years oiling the smooth periods of his panegyric or of the Roman epic poets of the Silver Age, who produced those vast and devastated poems with an imitative conformity almost Chinese to their great master Virgil; and for modern instances of Classicism, of Pope and of Racine.

Against this attitude there rises in eternal revolt the spirit which may be called Romantic, which cares not for tradition but originality, not for form, but colour. It realises the value, which extreme Classicism forgets, of spontaneity instead of restraint, of freedom instead of the bondage of law, of self-expression rather than self-control, of emotional and passionate sincerity in art rather than cunning of technique. Classicism, in the words of Pericles, "loves beauty with economy"; Romanticism loves beauty with ecstasy, without sparing, without economy, without reservations. It cares not for faultlessness, for avoiding mistakes, for not doing certain things; it cares for reaching the heights, for climax, and never minds the bathos, the depths. The Classicist cries with Ben Jonson of Shakespeare "'He never blotted a line' say you. I say 'Would he had blotted a thousand!'" but the Romanticist believes with Napoleon "That if one does not make mistakes, one makes nothing," with Bernard Shaw "That the poet has a right to have his chain tested by its strongest link." So must a Wordsworth be judged.

Romanticism, to conclude, cares for heart more than head, passion than intellect; it creates spontaneously, uncritically, unselfconsciously. It is the essence of Youth against the essence of Maturity, the Many in Greek philosophic language against the One, the Spirit of Dionysus in Nietzsche's phrase against the Spirit of Apollo.

Think of the history of the struggle. The naturalism of the Mycenaean civilisation before Homer is overlaid by the strict Geometric restraint of the invading and pervading North; the best Greek Art, as the best Art, I believe, always, is compounded of both freedom and law; but decadence brings dissolution. In Euripides the perfect bloom of Greek tragic form passes away with the gradual pushing of the Chorus out of the Action, the Greek tragic spirit tints from its marble purity to the colours of Romanticism. Love begins to set foot on the altar of Dionysus. Such a play is his *Andromeda*, now lost save in fragments, which opened with the maiden chained in the dim of dawn beside a faery, monster-haunted

sea and which, in Lucian's mocking phrase, in after-days so
bewitched the good folk of Abdera, town far-famed for its
stupidity, that the city was filled with seven-day old tragedians,
pale and haggard, chanting aloud "O Love, high monarch
over gods and men"[1]. That new influence descends through
Alexandria and the Greek novelists of later centuries to the
torrent of fiction that roars like Niagara over the bookstalls
of to-day.

The Muses passed to Rome. Imitative from its cradle,
though with a ponderous massiveness all its own, Roman
literature after the Augustan age became Classical à outrance.
Then the Barbarians, the Dark Ages, Medievalism and again
the fresh mating of the Classic and Romantic spirit in the
Renaissance.

For a picture highly imaginative, yet in its deep essentials
true, of the Classical spirit, latent and biding its time of
resurrection through the darkest hours of barbarism, we may
turn for a moment to Chesterton's *Ballad of the White Horse*.
There, among the leaders Alfred musters for the great fight
at Ethandune with Danish barbarism flooding in from the
North Sea, the poet has added, beside Saxon and Celt, a last
descendant of the race, whose eagles left Britain for ever four
centuries before, a last scion of Classic Rome—Mark of Italy.

> His fruit trees stood like soldiers
>   Drilled in a straight line.
> His strange stiff olives did not fail
> And all the kings of the earth drank ale,
>   But he drank wine.

---

[1] Courtney in his *Idea of Tragedy* points out that Andromeda's words
to Perseus:
> "Take me, O stranger, for thine handmaiden,
>   Or wife, or slave,"
are exactly Miranda's to Ferdinand in the most romantic of Shakespeare's
plays (*Tempest*, III, 2, 83-6).

Wide over wasted British plains
  Stood never an arch or dome,
Only the trees to toss and reel,
The tribes to bicker, the beasts to squeal,
But the eyes in his head were strong like steel,
  And his soul remembered Rome.

He may be historically impossible; spiritually he is very
symbolic. He was to fall at Ethandune; but he and his were
to mould the English spirit of seven hundred years onward.
We owe so much to these "whose souls remembered Rome."
And when we come to trace the descent of the greatest
Elizabethan drama from, on the one hand the formless,
childishly spontaneous and shapeless effusions of the Miracle-
play, on the other the meticulously rigid Senecan drama, like
Gorboduc, and the University Latin play, with their five acts,
their Chorus, their stereotyped conventions, their attempts to
cling even to the Unities of Time and Place, it may be more
apparent why we have dwelt so long on Classic and Romantic.

But, to begin at last at the beginning of all things with a
brief sketch of Seneca's Greek predecessors, we must picture
the first home of Tragedy; the heroic age of golden Mycenae
has vanished under one of those periodic waves of Northern
barbarism which for thousands of years swept down on the
Mediterranean lands; only after centuries the waters of the
cataclysm begin to recede. The Greece of Hesiod is one of
those "deserts called peace." Little fighting in Hesiod's
Boeotia, only the wearier aftermath of war—scarcity, want,
the anarchy, the class-hatred of peasants writhing under a
feudal baronage of gift-devouring kings. The world is grown
smaller as well as meaner; without sea communication travel-
ling has never been light work in Greece; and the sea is one
of Hesiod's ultimate horrors. There in his own mountain-
girdled plain, generation after generation, "man comes and
tills the soil and lies beneath." Those who venture out across

the sea, go pushed by dissension and over-population, to return no more, like the emigrants from Scotland after the '45 and from Ireland long after. Through the eighth and seventh centuries Greece spreads to East and West; but the dawn comes slowly from the sunrise. Echoes of the great things of the Orient, like the fall of Nineveh, reverberate dimly westward. Then the light spreads on to the islands of the Aegean. The Lyric poetry of Archilochus, Alcaeus, the fiery self-realisation of the individual, springs up; and philosophy arises in Ionia. And yet the boy Aeschylus born about 525 B.C. in an Athens without political freedom, with little art except a still rude sculpture and an immature vase-painting, with little literature of its own, save the poems of the genial old politician Solon and Thespis' first rude development of parochial religious drama, can never have dreamed, in the coldness of that dawn, of the noonday he was to live to see.

In his youth the Greek drama was still a strange, unlicked, shapeless thing—only freshly emancipated from a religion to which it had been as closely tied as the analogous Medieval miracle-play.

Now to precisely what sort of religion, without raising a hornet's nest of discussion, one cannot clearly say: it does not seem to matter vastly. Whether the dancing and mimicry of early drama was in honour of a vegetation Year-Daemon or the spirit of a buried king, is still a subject of undecided and acrimonious conflict. A rash attempt to reconcile the jarring alternatives might suggest that from the particular one passed to the general, from the soul of one dead king, still making his people's crops grow green in spring, to the universal power that makes all Nature revive and bud again. But all, or more than all, that is known in favour of what seems to me the likelier hypothesis will be found in Sir W. Ridgeway's *Origin of Tragedy*.

We must picture as persisting age after immemorial age, in the lonely villages, the little hill cities of Hellas, perched between peak and peak, or nestling between the mountains and the sea, these dances of sunburnt rustics—dances with strange chants and weird figures, and yet already with that inscrutable grace of all things Greek. Gradually as the custom grows older, as the generations of glad dancers pass into silence and their children glorify the powers of life and death in their brief turn,—gradually the religious intensity dies away, and the art of the conscious artist comes stealing into its place. The dance ceases to be felt as an impassioned appeal to friendly or terrible forces of the unseen world; we dance now because it always has been done; it is custom; and what a good custom it is! And to make it even better, we find someone, fellow-townsman or stranger, who has the feel and the gift, someone to whom the Muses can whisper beauty, to make us new dances and to better the old. Masters of the ballet arise; the century 650–550 B.C. sees Arion at Corinth, Alcman teaching the girls of Sparta his songs of wistful loveliness, the splendid and sonorous Stesichorus striking an epic lyre in Western Sicily. Beside the individual lyric of Aeolia, of Alcaeus and Sappho, stands now the lyric of the choir.

But in Attica there follows a new development. Athens is growing in peace and prosperity under the benevolent despotism of Pisistratus, gathering her strength in silence for the hectic and glorious centuries of liberty to come. King Theseus five hundred years before had made the territorial unity of Attica; Pisistratus was now to make it spiritual. He brought in Zeus the Olympian to dominate the petty local gods of his turbulent nobles; he brought in a greater still, Homer; and it must have been at least with his approval that under Thespis about 535 B.C. the village drama of the local cult found its centre too beside the shrine of Dionysus, below the Acropolis of Athens.

For the village dance of Attica had become Drama indeed. Tradition says it was Thespis, though it may have been some earlier and forgotten worthy, who in the interval while his dancers rested came forward and declaimed to the audience himself—the first of actors. Nor was he limited to monologue; he could engage in converse with the leader of his chorus. Ghost, hero, tyrant, messenger, God—he could be all by turns. The addition of further actors was merely a matter for time and his successors.

He did not rest there—probably his fame spread—it was easier for Thespis and his troupe to tour Attica than for Attica to tramp to Thespis' native Icaria, as Europe goes to Oberammergau. As to the local Medieval Mystery with its amateur resident actors succeeded the Morality with its professionals, so in the latter sixth century, Thespis packed his itinerant troupe on to a waggon and trundled off to conquer the world. He did not have to wander far—where one sits to-day with one's back to the rock of Athene's hill and the morning sun shining over Hymettus and the sea, there under Dionysus' patronage, Attic Drama found its home. Thespis had passed; and the next generation of tragedians was passing, when the first play of Aeschylus appeared about 500 B.C.

So, like the Medieval drama, only with far swifter development, the Greek drama passed from the domain of religion to that of art.

But Aeschylus does remain dominantly religious in tone. There is no time to dwell at length on the Greek Tragedians; they concern us here for their influence on Rome. But one may briefly say that Aeschylus is concerned with justifying God's ways; Sophocles with portraying man's, with humanity for its own sake; Euripides with impugning God's ways, and with Humanitarianism. Aeschylus the prophet, the soldier of the Great War who found Athens becoming estranged, as a generation grew up that knew neither him nor it, wrestling with the problem of World-governance alone like a Hebrew prophet, was to shake from his shoes his native dust and die among the Sicilian cornfields in the West.

Sophocles reigned in his stead. Of him, though perfectly happy in his life and in his work, there is not much to say, for our purpose. The perfect artist seldom rears great successors. He comes at the end of a line of development, which he brings to its climax of excellence; so that in his particular line little remains to be done. Sophocles remains there, in Mr Wells' words of our own dead friends, "rounded off and bright and done,"—to be equalled in his way by none, to be appreciated, even, only by the most sensitive among future generations.

With Euripides we come to the really vital influence on the tragedy of Rome from Ennius to Seneca. The Tragic Muse has passed from her splendid prime to the thoughtfulness and wistfulness of middle-age; the rift has begun within the lute; and in all the haunting melody of Euripides, in his tragic pathos—"most tragic of the poets"—in his passionate outcry against the world that Sophocles had found full of wonder and terror, but of beauty most of all, in all this wild protest, this insistent questioning, this hopeless regret of the last of the great tragedians, there sounds one perpetual note of dissonance; "one little grain of conscience makes him sour."

One must realise the man living through a twenty-eight years' war with his ideals being tortured into hypersensitive agony by the meannesses, and the basenesses of a desperate struggle for victory. The Heavens are iron above him; the gods the devils of superstition; he turns to humanity. And he finds nothing but a contemporary earth as hopelessly wrong as heaven. He cannot forget the oppressed and the neglected—women and slaves. He grows embittered. Perfect art means that intellect and emotion have kissed and go hand in hand in its creator's soul. Euripides, soured a little in the battle of scepticism, tends at times to become an intellectual, to make his characters talk rhetoric, be sophistic, too clever, too hardly brilliant; on the other side, his emotion, his intense and noble pity, tends, as to-day with Galsworthy it tends, to bury itself in a pathos too painful, in situations too realistically miserable, in a forgetfulness of any side of life but its ever-present unhappiness, nay, its horrors.

None the less it was, quite naturally, not Sophocles the perfect poet, but Euripides the thinker, the questioner, the cosmopolitan, "the human," who influenced the more sterile ages that followed, while tragedy ran dry and the mantle of Euripides descended on Menander, the great poet of the New Comedy. It was Euripides, again, who first godfathered the infant stage of Rome. For of the great Tragedians of the Republic, on the whole, Ennius, the earliest, is most influenced by Euripides, Pacuvius by Sophocles, Accius by Aeschylus; that is, the earliest Romans by the latest Greeks and *vice versa*. Then a century and a half after Accius, Seneca reverts utterly to Euripides.

Let us dwell for a moment on the distinctive and infectious things in the style of Euripides.

Firstly the Tragic Chorus as handled by him already bears on it the mark of its ultimate destiny, extinction. These descendants of our rustic dancers, once supreme, from the moment that Tragedy really begins, are throughout its history slowly and surely dominated and evicted by the actors. But Euripides was the first definitely to make these its creatures—who were in fact an incongruous anachronism forced only by religious convention on his modernist drama—to make them sing lyrics irrelevant to the immediate action, to convert them from an acting to an orchestral part, to turn them into an extra, providing musical interludes between acts.

We shall find the tendency carried even further by Seneca; not only are his lyrics often quite dissociated from their context; but the Chorus, seems already, as in Elizabethan drama, to be absent from the scene, between its recitations. Its resurrection in sixteenth century England was to be still more brief and futile; the sage and ancient men of Britain in *Gorboduc*, Andrea's ghost and Revenge in the *Spanish Tragedy* are feeble substitutes destined to perish without offspring. And yet some of us may remember having found the Chronicler in *Abraham Lincoln* by no means unsatisfactory.

Next there is the ghost. He is very probably the oldest figure in tragedy—the dead hero about whose grave the chorus danced. The ghost of Clytemnestra opens the *Eumenides* of Aeschylus; Darius is raised in his *Persae*; but it is to the Euripidean ghost, such as the wraith of Polydorus in the prologue of the *Hecuba*, and the apparition of Achilles described in the *Troades*, that the spectres of Seneca are really akin—the ghost of Tantalus which begins the *Thyestes*, that of Thyestes which introduces the *Agamemnon*,—phantoms which were to propagate and fill the Tudor stage to repletion. From them descend not merely august figures like Hamlet's ghost and Andrea's, but the legions of dead through whom the living characters of minor Elizabethans elbow an unconcerned way, for example, the five ghosts who execute a dance in the *Revenge of Bussy d'Ambois*, the six who together with one villain and two sub-villains, so richly furnish forth the tragedy of *Perfidus Hetruscus*.

So it is with other stock Senecan characters. Juliet's nurse goes back through the Senecan hag (there are two nurses in the *Octavia* alone) to the old women of the *Hippolytus* and the *Medea*, who in turn recall that very Shakespearian figure, Orestes' nurse, in the *Choephoroe* of Aeschylus.

Again, the Senecan tyrant, prototype of the villains of melodrama, is an obvious descendant of the Euripidean

Menelaus and Lycus. The Roman takes the figures of the Greek, remoulds them with his own clumsy, massive violence, repaints them with his own crude loudness. The nuances, the half-tones perish; but one still can recognise the pedigree of the vulgarised and coarsened Senecan despot.

As with the characters, so with the ideas and emotions of Euripides. The pathos of "the most tragic of the poets" becomes the hysteria of Seneca. The agonies in Euripides, if sometimes slightly piled on, as in the *Troades*, are still those of pity, not of terror. It was merely characteristic of the Roman mind that the emotionalism of pity in the Greek poet should become a cult of horror in Seneca.

There remains that opposite side of Euripides—Euripides the intellectual, the pupil of Anaxagoras, the friend of Socrates, the student writing away from the bustle of the Philistine world in his sea-cave looking out on Salamis.

The love of reasoning, the influence of the sophists with their art of persuasion, their rhetoric, fills his plays with speeches and debates, pleadings and counter-pleadings, cut-and-thrust retort and repartee. It was natural for Quintilian to find in Euripides the poet *par excellence* of the future orator; it was also Romanly typical of Seneca to ape what is, if sometimes a fault, yet a striking fault in the Greek, until it becomes a staccato absurdity in the Latin.

With the rhetoric goes the love of epigrammatic moralising. The Greek loved the proverbial wisdom on which his youth was nurtured, the maxims, so simple and so profound, of the immemorial wise. But once more it was Euripides above all who provided the happy hunting ground of the compilers of commonplace books. On the sins of women and the sins against them, on the iniquity of established deities and established despotisms, on the wisdom and the follies of love he provided a mine of maxims. Here, as ever, the Roman imitated by exaggerating. Practical and matter-of-fact, he loved compendious wisdom even better than the Greek—but it must be worldly wisdom, something not pure, but to be applied straight to common rounds and daily tasks.

For follow the history of a Greek philosophy like Stoicism to Rome—you will find its metaphysics, its logic, everything that has not a practical bearing on life, ruthlessly shed; till only its ethics, converted into a business and week-day morality, remain. Hence while Euripidean tragedy is rich in general maxims and thoughts about men and things, but, in most cases, thoughts which need thinking over and maxims which are often real poetry, Senecan tragedy, to the delight of the Elizabethans, pullulates with epigrams neither deep nor brilliant, but pointed and polished to look as if they were.

Such are some of the bequests of Euripides to those future ages for which he was of such far greater appeal than his elders, Sophocles and Aeschylus. Senecan irrelevance of chorus, Senecan ghosts and stock characters, Senecan melodrama, Senecan rhetoric and epigram, are inherited by Rome from Euripides, as they were to be handed on by Seneca in turn to the Renaissance.

With Euripides the race of Greek Tragedy was run: it staggers on indeed into the fourth century: but senile and moribund.

Before we turn to Rome, as the light spreads ever westward, let us look back a moment in retrospect. Tragedy has arisen and bloomed and perished in her first incarnation. From the band of mumming yokels, dancing before the village saint or for the village ritual of fertility, whichever it may be, by the virtue of that one fertile idea by which between their songs the poet breaks into dialogue with the leader of the chorus, almost in the course of a generation has arisen a drama great as any in history.

Religion has faded; Art has stepped into her place. From

Aeschylus wrestling, as Jacob in Penuel, in the empyrean with
God, and Sophocles watching steadily the beauty and the
majesty, the pity and the terror of humanity, Tragedy has passed
to Euripides with his grey disillusion stealing across the older
dreams, and the sharp discords of pain shrilling through the
older harmonies. She has come down from Heaven to Earth;
Euripides has taken her and put on her lips the cunning
speech of common men, and on her once heroic stature the
rags of poverty and wretchedness; her loveliness dominated
even these; but the last master is dead, and straightway she
is gone[1].

A century passes; the Greek spirit goes on to conquer
other worlds—Plato dreams, Demosthenes thunders. Philip
of Macedon, beloved of Mr Wells, crushes in his mailed hand
the last faded flowers of Greek liberty; in its dead name, his
son enslaves a world. But Greece had lost her soul. Called
after him, Alexandria arises—the academic, the scholarly, the
sophisticated—with its hot-house orchids of literature, and
its aviaries of exotic poets, twittering erudition. The greatness
of the fifth century has disintegrated into the Romance of
an Apollonius, the pedantic classicism of a Lycophron. Half
a century more passes; Greece tosses in her fitful sleep under
the weight of Macedon; Alexandria still twitters. But to
westward Rome, five centuries before a mere stronghold of
banditti above the plains of Latium, has mastered Italy, with
its Greek cities in the South, and after twenty-three years of
agonized war wrested from the Phoenician, her first province,
Greek Sicily.

In the next year, 240 B.C., appears the first sign of the
Greek leaven working in that strange lump. Livius Andronicus, a Greek of Tarentum, enslaved when his city fell

[1] So the characters of Chinese drama in process of time steadily
descended the social scale from demi-gods to heroes, then to mandarins,
then to physicians and tradesmen, and finally by the thirteenth century
to labourers and artisans (cf. Menander).

in his childhood, then a schoolmaster, produces his first plays, a tragedy and a comedy, in Rome.

The second incarnation of Tragedy has begun.

Roman tragedy is an elusive subject; for the obvious reason that except for Seneca, child of a later and utterly different period, it has perished, all but fragments. It used to be assumed that, because it perished, it deserved to; those were the days of a comfortable belief which extended the Survival of the Fittest to Classical Literature. As Pichon[1] points out, this quite false assumption of the worthlessness of Roman republican tragedy gave rise to mushroom crops of explanation of the said worthlessness. "Roman tragedy dealt with foreign legends, uninteresting to the populace"; so did a vast quantity of Elizabethan drama. "Rome was too fond of gladiatorial shows"; so was Spain, replies Pichon, of bull-fights; and yet Calderon exists; and was not Elizabethan tragedy cradled in the very cock-pits and bear-gardens themselves?

As a matter of fact those priceless possessions the letters of Cicero[2] give a vivid idea of the still vital influence of Tragedy on the Roman populace, even when Accius, the last great tragedian had already been dead a quarter of a century. And this though almost from the first the Senate had shown itself as stepmotherly towards the stage as the Authorities of Elizabethan London. For the drama was regarded as a disseminator of Greek decadence and the Greeks were still feared bearing gifts.

So it must have been merely on a temporary wooden staging that on that eventful day of the Ludi Romani of 240 B.C. appeared the two plays of Andronicus. Drama of a rude and rustic sort was familiar enough to its audience—such as the Bucolicisms of wrangling peasants of the Campagna, the so-called 'Fescennine' consisting of "échanges de sottises

---

[1] *Histoire de la Littérature Latine*, 42–3.   [2] E.g. *Ad Atticum*, II, 19, 3.

rustiques," the 'Satura' distinguished by having a rudi-
mentary plot, the Atellanae perhaps of Campanian origin
with their stock characters, Maccus and Bucco, like Devil
and Vice in the Medieval Morality. Players, too, had been
brought from Etruria to placate the gods into staying a
plague. But as in England, so in Italy, though comedy was
in some degree indigenous, tragedy came from without. And
this was the first time Greek culture set foot on the Roman
stage; a Greek barbarised, no doubt, almost out of recogni-
tion, but still Greek. One can imagine that grim nobility,
iron-grey generals grown old in twenty-five years of war, a
little scornful, a little curious, a little distrustful of this strange
Muse from overseas, even if some of them had perhaps
already seen tragedies in the conquered Greek cities of the
West; the background is filled with the Roman commons,
stout, brawny, simple, open-mouthed.

Picture that audience; in the next two centuries it is to
change a great deal, like the City herself. Those blunt minds
are to become both more cultured and more coarse, those
brown burly hands both whiter and more cruel. But that
character in its massiveness corrodes slowly; and that
character one must understand to understand the tragedy of
Rome. For Greece is sweetness, Rome strength, Greece is
nerve, and Rome muscle, Greece genius and intellect, Rome
talent and character, Greece the Parthenon, Rome the
Colosseum, Greece youth, and Rome middle-age. The very
lands that bred them keep their stamp to this day. You
may leave one night the sharp crags of Epirus red in the
westering sun, the land of poverty and clear thought, of little
lonely valleys and all-enlacing sea, of sharp and crystal outline,
peaks silhouetted with dazzling definition against a steel clear
sky; and land in the dark at Brindisi and see dawn shimmer
up across the soft white dust of Apulia, and midday kissing
the green highlands and little quiet glens of Samnium, and

afternoon throwing its long shadows lovingly across the fat
tilth of Campania, and sunset over the lush peacefulness of
the hill-girt Volscian land, till the lights of Rome glimmer to
Northward against the dark mantle Night has flung on dim
Etruria. And all day long under those different forms you
will, if you look, find the same spirit of Italy in its unity—that
unity itself a thing which Greece has not. You will feel in
the presence of a kindlier land, the Saturnian mother Virgil
sings, fosterer of sons stronger if less nimble, more stalwart
if less clever, hard but with a gentler feeling of love for this
Nature of their native earth than most Greeks had. For Love
is not the feeling inspired by the crags of Taygetus as one
struggles across the/hills from Kalamata or by the sight of
misty Geraneia and Helicon and Parnassus, towering into
the heaven of heavens above the Corinthian gulf, or of
Cyllene with the sunlight dazzling on the snows of spring.
Even the great Greek nature-poet Theocritus was a Sicilian.

But to get back from scenery to the stage. It is only what
we should expect, that Roman adaptations of Greek drama
should make its maxims more particular and definitely
practical than "Nothing too much," less spiritual than
"Know thyself," its rhetoric far more rhetorical—(for Latin
oratory does almost gain as much in sonorousness as it loses
in subtlety)—its horrors and passions stronger and cruder,
its pity and its lamentation more stoical and less womanly,
while adding that feeling for natural beauty which made even
the plutocrats of Rome scatter their villa-palaces over the
fairest sites of Italy. The Roman mind is narrower, less
many-sided than the Greek; it runs a few things hard. And
Seneca was to be even narrower and more restricted and
over-emphatic than the Republicans. These differences
matter for our purpose; it was because Roman tragedy was
cruder and stronger and less delicate that all Seneca was
translated into English by 1581, while the next classical

dramatist to be so completed, Sophocles, had to wait nearly two hundred years longer, till 1759. That is a fact to remember in the history of classical influence; it signifies worlds.

Now typical of the Roman mind is Roman religion, that business man's creed, its dignified but sharp dealing with the gods, its dislike of 'superstitio,' that is, the folly of the man who pays Heaven more for its favours than one need; the priests are almost secular, they can hold most offices of state like any other man; they are little more than the state's religious solicitors. The gods themselves are shadowy; none of the dazzlingly beautiful and clear-cut offspring of the Greek imagination; not the young Apollo, but abstractions, strange for this concrete people, Fides, Concordia, Pudicitia. But it is very Roman really. This division of labour is useful; and it is essential to be precisely accurate about addressing the right god for one's purpose[1].

After the gods the lesser sanctities of hearth and home; again we find the same scrupulous observance of the ties of blood and kin, of ancestry, of ancestral custom, of proud conservatism. Our terms of praise are 'progressive,' 'advanced,' 'up-to-date': the Roman—'priscus,' 'antiquus'— old-fashioned, of the good old type. Rome is as Pichon says "classique d'instinct"; one and the same spirit dwells incarnate in Varro's *Antiquities* and Virgil's *Aeneid*.

No less characteristic of the Roman mind is the Latin language itself; shrewd not subtle, forcible not fine, great in its organ-voiced sonority, its supreme magnificence in "le style lapidaire." Small wonder that Dr Johnson in the teeth of all the *élite* of London, persisted that his epitaph on Goldsmith should be in Latin. It is the utterance of human

---

[1] Cf. Pater, *Marius the Epicurean*. "Vaticanus who causes the infant to utter his first cry, Fabulinus who prompts his first word, Cuba who keeps him quiet in his cot, Domiduca especially, for whom Marius had through life a particular memory and devotion, the goddess who watches over one's safe-coming home."

will. But the strongest wills do not go with the keenest brains.

Thus among the first written poems in Latin was the work of old Appius Claudius the censor. It is finely in character that already one of the very few surviving fragments should be

> Faber fortunae unusquisque est suae.
> "Each man is his own fortune's architect."

In short, Rome's conquest of the Greek world was the conquest of brain by will.

One has to remember finally, that, not surprisingly, poetry came late to these people, and from without; and was scantly honoured when it did. Even Philology is eloquent here. The word 'poesis' had been borrowed with the thing itself from Greece: and to the early poets was applied an offensive name 'grassatores,' idle rogues, while their work was regarded as mere trifling. Again, the professional actor was classed with the auctioneer and undertaker as a pariah, though Roscius and Aesopus did indeed attain eminent respectability towards the close of the Republic and the position of actors generally improved under the Empire. Such were the conditions of the Drama at Rome.

It remains to sketch the actual tragedy of the Republic.

Of Livius Andronicus there is little more to be said. His translation of the *Odyssey* into Saturnians, not his plays, was his *magnum opus*, compared by Cicero to the archaic statues attributed to Daedalus; but Horace still had his works flogged into him by the hefty Orbilius.

Naevius, 269–199, Latin peasant, dour, bitter, satirical to the point of getting himself into serious trouble, but a man in whom the genuine Roman 'gravitas' rings loud and true, produced his first play five years after Andronicus in 235. He also invented a new type of drama, based on Roman history instead of Greek legend and comparable to the English Chronicle Play; of these so-called *Praetextae* or *Plays of the Purple Stripe*, the much later *Octavia* is our only surviving instance.

Two lines of Naevius which survive sum the man.

> Semper pluris feci potioremque ego
> Libertatem multo habui quam pecuniam.

> "Ever I valued and esteemed far more
> Freedom than gold."

He lived long in prison and died in exile thanks to it.

We come now to the great Roman trinity, Ennius (239–169), Pacuvius (220–130), Accius (170–86), of whom, as we have said, Ennius is nearest Euripides, because it was inevitable that Euripides, the cosmopolitan, the romantic, should at first outstrip his more difficult rivals in influencing barbarian Rome, as Seneca outstripped the Greeks in Renaissance England.

Ennius, though his work only survives in fragments, retains for us a personality strangely emphatic and clear. Comparisons, where not odious are frequently inept; but he does bear a certain likeness to Marlowe. For he stands, not at the very beginning of his national tragedy, but so near, that his great and revolutionary influence affected its whole development, as Marlowe's did Elizabethan drama. Again, Ennius (though this concerns Epic, not Drama), killed the Saturnian by his successful naturalisation of the Greek hexameter; Marlowe assured the supersession of rhyme by the classically-derived blank verse of *Tamburlaine*; in both cases we have an early and intensely national poet enriching his national literature by wise adaptation of the foreignly derived. Both have, like Seneca, the love for grandiosity, and bombast not only of thought but also of style and diction; whereas the later Seneca with all his hyperbole, does not indulge in *sesquipedalia verba*; he may stagger the imagination, he seldom fills the mouth.

But hear Ennius; where Euripides says quietly,

Κορίνθιαι γυναῖκες, ἐξῆλθον δόμων.

"Women of Corinth, I have left the house,"

he thunders,

O quae Corinthi arcem altam habetis, matronae opulentae
    optimates.

"Dwellers in Corinth's towering citadel,
Ladies of great possessions, lineage high."

So his Orestes swears,

                Per ego deum sublimas subices
Umidas, unde oritur imber sonitu saevo et spiritu.

"By the tall cloud-drenched firmament of God
Whence springs the wild tempest with shrill blasts of storm."

Once more the frankness of Ennius (I wear, he says, my loves and hates upon my face), his passion and enjoyment of the pleasures of life (such that, in Rabelais' words, "some sneaking jobbernol alleged his verses smelt more of wine than of the lamp"), his mixture of Epicurean scepticism and enthralled speculation about the mysteries of things, which involved him in Pythagoreanism—all these traits have their counterparts in the outspoken atheist, the tavern-brawler, the sceptical yet fascinated author of *Dr Faustus*. Only fortune willed that the one should die merry and gouty at three score and ten, the other be stabbed in a tavern brawl over bought kisses in his prime. As for the philosophising strain we shall find hereafter in Seneca with his Stoic babes in arms, it is already here; only Ennius is Epicurean. He laughs at the soothsayers, the charlatans, the astrologers who knew better the way of the stars than of their slipshod feet. He denies that the gods care for a weary world, where right-

eousness is wretched and wrong prospers. He loves a man:
he has the dignity of one. Witness his own true epitaph:

Nemo me dacrumis decoret nec funera fletu
Faxit. Cur? volito vivus per ora virum.
"No tears for me, no pomp of funeral train.
Why? I live still upon the lips of men."

His successor Pacuvius was the son of Ennius' sister:
learned even to pedantry, he tried strange tricks with his
native tongue, spawning monstrous clusters of compound
words.

Nerei repandirostrum, incurvicervicum pecus.

He shows a similar scepticism and rationalism and mocks
at the haruspices and their inspections of the entrails of
sacrificial victims.

Nam isti qui linguam avium intelligunt
Plusque ex alieno iecore sapiunt quam ex suo,
Magis audiendum quam auscultandum censeo.
"Why as for those who know the speech of birds
And learn more from a sheep's heart than their own,
They should be rather heard than listened to."

But he shows a more tiresome philosophicalness—witness
long disquisitions on the nature of Fortune and of the
Aether. He is one of those naive creatures who insist in
writing the commentary to their own texts and, worse still,
in the body of their texts. In fact, he is not in himself vastly
interesting. The natural stoicism of his characters is his
nearest bond with Seneca. Such is the dictum in his *Ulysses*:

Conqueri fortunam adversam non lamentari licet.
"'Tis right to regret ill-fortune, not bewail it."

It is all a little inhuman.

Accius, the last of the three great Republican dramatists,
was born in 170; in his style there is something Aeschylean,

and in him the Latin sonorousness is more marked than ever;
his "high spirit" was the characteristic that struck Horace
and Ovid about him. Seneca has clearly read his *Atreus*.
And some of his choral anapaests, if they were less virile and
intense and strong might pass for Seneca's. These are some
typical fragments, all too brief:

> En impero Argis; sceptra mi liquit Pelops
> Qua ponto ab Helles atque ab Ionio mari
> Urgetur Isthmos,

(lines, if not his, very much in his style).

> "Lo, I am lord of Argos; Pelops left
> Me sceptred king where upon either hand
> The deep of Helle and the Ionian sea
> Press hard the Isthmus."

> Apud abundantem amnem et rapidas undas Inachi.

> "There by the ancient mighty river, the whirling waves of
> Inachus."

> Sub axe posita ad stellas septem, unde horrifer
> Aquilonis stridor gelidas molitur nives.

> "Beneath the Pole and nigh the Seven Stars
> Whence the wild whistle of the north wind hurls
> The bitter snow."

> Simul et circum merga sonantibus
> Excita saxis saeva sonando
> Crepitu clangente cachinnat.

> "And the startled gull that wheels on high,
> As the rocks resound with the sound of dread,
> Laughs out its clamorous cry."

> Forte ante Auroram radiorum argutam indicem
> Cum e somno in segetem agrestis cornutos ciet
> Ut rorulentas terras ferro fumidas
> Proscindant.

> "Ere Dawn arises, day's bright harbinger,
> What time the ploughman calls his team afield
> To break the steaming fallows wet with dew."

One feels one could gladly have sacrificed Seneca to bring back Accius from the dead. The ultimate indefinable quality which makes poetry, which one wants without knowing what one wants on almost every page of Seneca, starts here from every line. The verse, too, runs like a torrent, like his own "ancient mighty river," with the words crashing upon one another like fir-tree boles in the headlong flood; while Seneca with his silver Latin smoothness, his eschewing of elision, slides turbidly and greasily along.

After Accius Roman tragedy dwindles—performances went on, but writers grew more and more academic. Julius Caesar produced an *Oedipus*; Cicero's brother four tragedies in a fortnight in the exhilarating air of Britain; Varius a *Thyestes*, Ovid a *Medea*. But times had changed; taste grew depraved; the Roman stage was swamped in magnificent pageantry, in Drury Lane effects; when liberty ceased, serious public representations might seem dangerous to an emperor; Greek legends were full of tyrants, allusions were bound to be invented by the audience if not by the poet; the public stage grew wholly frivolous, with its mimes and pantomimes, its bloodshed and lust. Perhaps like Lorenzo de' Medici the emperors saw the political merits of public frivolity.

Roman tragedy was dimmed; but its effects must not be slurred: they have left their mark on Lucretius and Virgil; they doubtless left it still more on the public of Lucretius and Virgil, by the humanising influence of Greek legend and Greek culture. The torch of tragedy burnt but smokily in the heavy, thunderous atmosphere of Rome; but it was at least kept lighted there, and the vital flame preserved for nobler ages and lands of purer air.

CHAPTER II

SENECA THE MAN

THE Republic blustered to its end, and passed in a death-agony of twenty years of civil slaughter. War-weary, broken in spirit, craving no longer self-government, but government at any price, no longer liberty, but at least law, the exhausted world turned to rest with a sigh of gratitude under the shadow of Augustus' quiet sovereignty. In those years when Peace was new and enthusiasm fresh, while the virility of the old turbulent republic still ran strong and men felt that autocracy had crushed licence, not yet despotism liberty, arose the Golden Age of Roman Literature. It was as when, after long days of rain and tempest in the hills, suddenly bright weather comes and the sun makes glorious a hundred torrents foaming down in spate with storm-fed waters and all nature looks her fairest. But, as the sun shines on day after day, the waters dwindle and the live green withers and all grows hard and dim and dusty; so also the inspiration and magnificence of the first Augustans was to fade little by little through frivolous sparkle to the death-blank sterile silence of Tiberius' day.

About four years after Horace died, were born at opposite ends of the Empire, the one at Corduba in the far West, the other at Bethlehem in Judea, perhaps the most typical and the most original characters of the first century A.D.

Seneca the Younger, will stand very well for the new imperial generation, as his father Seneca the Elder stood to the last for the age that was dying: he and his sons, especially the two younger, made one of those families where there is much sympathy, but not understanding. Understanding between generations is indeed rare at any time: it may be that the Chinese filial piety and the Chinese stagnation of past centuries were each part-cause and part-effect of the other: but in the Europe of the first century B.C. changing like wind-swept vapour into the Europe of the first A.D., little wonder if intellectually the children were against the fathers and the fathers against the children.

Seneca the Elder, born about 55 B.C., was of equestrian rank: he might, he laments, have heard Cicero, had not the Civil Wars kept him home in Spain: he may have held some post in the provincial civil service: but the capital was his spiritual home, and Roman rhetoric the delight of his soul; his vast knowledge of it is still his title to survive as an extant classic, and its decline since the golden days of Cicero was his perpetual grief. He seems to have spent much of his life pursuing this fading beauty in her Rome: he settled there with his family: and there he died, probably after Tiberius' death in 37 A.D., before his own son's exile in 41.

He married one Helvia, who bore him three sons, first M. Annaeus Novatus, the Gallio of the Acts and of Anatole France, second L. Annaeus Seneca, and third M. Annaeus Mela, father of the poet Lucan. It is not easy to picture her, which would be interesting, instead of her virtues, which are not, from her son's *Consolation* to her on his exile—a portrait only too like those crape-framed photographs of one's landlady's Victorian relatives. One imagines, however, a woman with much of the traditional Roman matron of good birth, with plenty of intelligence and with some culture; though her excellent but antiquated husband, who disliked equally blue-stockings and philosophers, forbade her more than a nodding acquaintance with the moral sciences. He was to find his offspring less malleable.

For, like most self-made men, he was particularly set on making his children's fortunes for them; and, as the successful do, he overrated the importance of success; he had risen in the world; they must go on rising. How? By the gift of persuasion, by Ciceronian oratory. Cicero, it is true, was buried forty years before the younger Seneca was born, and with him the brief day when the tongue could dream itself mightier than the sword; but one is slow to recognise that oneself and one's age are obsolete. The old Annaeus lived on, exploding intermittently at the degeneracy and limpness and effeminacy of this frivolous generation. The younger generation, however, did not share his illusions; oratory with one awful exception, the professional accusers, the bloodhounds of a Tiberius or a Domitian, was doomed to academicism and extinction. What is freedom of speech without freedom of action? And with Tiberius even freedom of speech was to cease its sham existence.

His three sons behaved exactly like the three sons in Fairy Tales; each went completely his own way and prospered, till the same violent end befell them all.

Novatus the eldest was to live most according to plan; he was to become, not indeed, a second Cicero, but a very eminent declaimer, to be adopted by the rhetorician Junius Gallio, under his brother's supremacy to become proconsul of Achaia, and after his brother's final fall to die by his own hand; he was also to be immortalised, in the Acts of the Apostles, for an insouciance caring about nothing, and in Dio Cassius[1] for a jest about which no one is likely now-a-days to care.

Annaeus Mela the youngest, on the other hand, preferred cash to credit, and that real power which could be enjoyed, as Atticus and Maecenas had shown, without rising above equestrian rank to the gaudy shams of obsolete offices. He served his Mammon faithfully to the death; by too insistent

---

[1] Dio Cassius, LX, 35. He said Claudius had been "hooked to Heaven" (the bodies of condemned criminals being so dragged away).

dunning of his son Lucan's debtors after that son's tragic
suicide he raised up an informer whose accusation of so fat
a victim was extremely grateful to Nero. So he too must
open his veins, leaving a will which threw a substantial sop
to Tigellinus and complained of the hardness of his fate
seeing that two other persons he named were still allowed to
live, though far more disloyal. One of them as a matter of fact,
had already been put to death: the other—which was presumably what Mela wanted—shortly afterwards was. So unamiable
relations may even the best conducted philosophers have.

Lucius, the second son, took a third and very different
direction. Imagine the offspring of a worldly and successful
newspaper proprietor turned violent Theosophist. He discovered in himself, as happens at that age, a soul, and with
fervour proceeded to its salvation. The enthusiasm of youth
is one of the best things in all the world; it is sometimes one
of the most tedious. So he sat at the feet of Sotion the
Pythagorean, who made a vegetarian of him, on the ground
that even if the soul of one's grandam might not haply
inhabit a bird, it was well to give her the benefit of the
doubt—besides being economical. For a year the young
convert ate no meat: and thought he found his brains the
clearer; but in 19 A.D. the Roman government, periodically
alarmed at the influx of Oriental superstitions, had one of its
intermittent witch-hunts. Eccentricities of diet were sus-
picious; and the elder Seneca, as the son relates with a
charm and humour one cannot always give him credit for,
did not have much difficulty in persuading him to dine better.
He made a desultory attack on rhetoric, but soon turned
back to the more congenial eloquence of philosophers.
About 20 A.D. he was following Attalus the Stoic, of whom
even in the letters of his old age he speaks with reverence
and affection. "When I heard him," he says, "declaiming
against the vices, errors and evils of life, often I pitied

mankind and thought him sublime and exalted above the summit of human worth." He returned to things mundane; but some traces of this sage's influence, he relates with honest pride, remained always with him—abstention from oysters, mushrooms, wine, vapour-baths and ointment.

But the young disciple was not possessed of a constitution to stand too much practical Stoicism; he practised, in the words of his most recent French biographer, "gross imprudences, such as cold baths in January"; his lungs became diseased, he wasted away. He grew so ill indeed, that he contemplated suicide, and only refrained out of consideration for his indulgent father. "For I considered," he says, "not with how much fortitude I could die, but with how little he would be able to bear my loss" (*Ep.* 78, 1). He attributes his recovery chiefly to the soothing study of philosophy—"I owe her my life, and that is the least of my debts." He appears next to have travelled to Egypt, where his devoted aunt, his mother's sister and wife of the prefect of Egypt, who had brought him from Spain to Rome as a child, nursed him through a dangerous illness. About 32 A.D. she returned with him to Rome, and after a shipwreck in which at the risk of her life she saved her drowned husband's body, by her influence secured her nephew the quaestorship (*c.* 33 A.D.). He married a wife. Tiberius died (37) and Caligula, at first with fairest promise, reigned in his stead. Seneca was already famed as a writer. As Ovid a generation earlier, he was born exactly in due time. His contemporaries, like Montaigne his admirer fifteen centuries later, yawned at the 'windiness' of Cicero. "I would not," says old Michel, "have an author make it his business to render me attentive: or that he should cry out thirty times *Oyez* as the heralds do." Their jaded palates wanted something sharp and pungent, wit and epigram, new and ever more sharply pointed ways of saying the old things. Seneca, with the uncanny ingenuity of an Ovid could hit their taste exactly, could fling the old period and the old style to the winds; Quintilian shaking his head in after years over his pernicious influence on the young writer, still grudgingly admits his brilliance.

Caligula was more grudging still; stark mad by this, but by no means an utter fool, he decried this new and rival eloquence as "mere prize-compositions" and "sand without lime." Jealous of a brilliant forensic speech delivered by Seneca in his hearing he would have applied the yet more trenchant criticism of the sword, if one of his mistresses had not persuaded him that this consumptive genius was too near death's door to be worth killing. But his intended victim was to outlive Caligula, and in revenge immortalise with the vivid touches of a contemporary many of that monster's bestialities[1]. In 41 A.D. Claudius succeeded his murdered nephew: but Seneca had only exchanged danger for disaster.

As befalls literary successes, he had become a carpet-lion in Roman salons; one imagines a pale, still youthful genius with hectic eye and forked tongue, discharging volleys of epigrams almost too superbly neat to be cheap, cherry-stones so consummately carved as to be all but real art. Perhaps he forgot the wagging beard of Attalus in that mundane, compulsorily frivolous society, that flippant world living under an intermittent terror and playing at its dangerous little jests and intrigues with sometimes life for stake. At all events he had sufficiently the air of having forgotten, to be accused and condemned for adultery with Julia, daughter of Germanicus and sister of Caligula.

Julia was twenty-three, young and beautiful. She had been seduced by her brother, then banished to an island on a

[1] As in that typical Senecan climax to a description of a nocturnal execution of some of Caligula's victims. "He had tormented them with all the agonies that nature knows, with pulleys and iron plates, with rack and flame, and with the sight of his own countenance."

charge of conspiracy. Recalled on the accession of her uncle Claudius (41 A.D.) she speedily roused the jealousy of the empress, Messalina, by the attraction she exercised on him. Augustus with a statesman's anxiety about the Roman birthrate and thence about Roman morality had made adultery a public offence by the Lex Julia of 18 B.C., a measure destined to be less prolific probably of babies than of professional informers. At all events the chaste Messalina found it a serviceable weapon: and Seneca was lighted on as the cat's paw to push the chestnut into the fire. He and Julia were accused and condemned; she was a second time banished to an island and shortly put to death; Seneca, sentenced to die but reprieved by Claudius, found himself eating the bitter bread of exile in barbarous Corsica. His likeness to Ovid, likewise the banished victim of the misconduct, true or false, of a Julia, was but too complete. As to his real guilt or innocence the judicious historian will save his own ink and his readers' time by owning at once that there is not enough evidence even for conjecture.

He was in his prime; he had lived, intensely and to the best of a considerable ability, in both worlds; he had won a first-rate literary position in spite of his ill-health, the *entrée* to the best society in Rome though only of provincial and equestrian birth; he had probably published by this time his treatises on India and Egypt, on Earthquakes, on Anger, his *Consolation to Marcia* on the death of her son and perhaps a certain amount of poetry. And now at the height of his brilliance he was snuffed out and left fuming in the evillest odour, just for a woman's feud.

However he put a brave face on his destiny. He would write still, study still; the same stars looked down on Corsica as on Rome; Nature was there as real and ready to reveal her secrets to her questioning sons. M. Waltz attributes to the beginning of his exile the treatises *On the Wise Man's*

Constancy and *On Providence*: but the one is also dated from Nero's time, the other from his second and last disgrace. So it is safer to confine oneself to the *Consolations* to his mother Helvia and to Polybius, in their bitter contrast, and the melancholy epigrams *On Exile*. His mother receives from him very much the commonplaces of comfort which Shakespeare's Bolingbroke must hear from his father and which Queen Anne's Bolingbroke has paraphrased in his own *Reflections upon Exile*.

> All places that the eye of Heaven visits,
> Are to a wise man ports and happy havens.

It is written, one feels, in a voice that quavers a little every now and then: the unhappy author is singing to keep his own courage up, and is trying to be not more consoler than consoled. He clings to pride: with a distant echo of Homer's trumpet-call:

> Κεῖσο μέγας μεγαλωστί.
> "Great you lay there and greatly fallen."

He proclaims indomitably: "If a great man falls, he is great when fallen."

But he was to follow the path of Ovid, to its querulous end. There he sat, perhaps where still stands on Cap Corse the medieval ruin called "Seneca's Tower"; on clear days he could see his Italy and in his beloved Virgil's words:

> Stretch hands of yearning toward the further shore.

A friend or two may have followed his exile; there would be a few government officials, a few soldiers; but he must have missed dismally the wit and intellect of Rome. He might have written as in "far Cathay" 800 years later the Chinese poet[1], banished in the service of soulless bureaucracy.

---

[1] Waley, 170 *Chinese Poems*, p. 152.

> The inhabitants of Pa resemble wild apes:
> Fierce and lusty they fill the mountains and the prairies.
> Among such as these I cannot hope for friends,
> And am pleased with anyone who is even remotely human.

He saw himself growing towards his fifties with silence and oblivion closing on him like a shroud. He broke into a wail of bitter despair.

> Corsica terribilis, quum primum incanduit aestas
> Saevior, ostendit quum ferus ora canis,
> Parce relegatis, hoc est iam parce sepultis.
> Vivorum cineri sit tua terra levis.

> "Corsica, isle of terror, when Summer first shines clear
> More savage still, when Sirius blazes high,
> O spare now him that's exiled, nay him that's buried here,
> Upon his living dust, O lightly lie."

> Non panis, non haustus aquae, non ultimus ignis;
> Hic sola haec duo sunt, exsul et exilium.

> "No bread, no water, not a funeral flame,
> Only the exile and his exile's shame."

Like Merlin spell-bound by Vivien within the hollow oak of Broceliande he lay "lost to use and life and name and fame." However, he bestirred his wits: at the end of two years, about 43 A.D., Polybius the freedman, literary secretary (*a studiis*) and master of the requests (*a libellis*) to Claudius, a creature of vague but vast influence, lost his younger brother. Seneca seized the opportunity to compose a *Consolation*, which should apply flattery, directly to the servant and indirectly to his master, as gross as even the stomach of a Roman emperor or a Roman freedman could stand. Dio Cassius says that in after years he tried to suppress his adulations of the freedman and of Messalina: in the latter instance he or Time has succeeded: the first remains.

"Lift up your heart," he writes to Polybius, "and when tears rise to your eyes turn them on Caesar: they will be dried by the spectacle of his great and resplendent divinity.

"Let that star which has shone out over a world hurled to the depths and plunged in gloom, be radiant for ever.

"O blessed is your clemency, Caesar! Which makes exiles live more tranquilly under you, than Rome's greatest lived under Gaius.

"Let Caesar decide how he shall judge my cause: his justice will see that it is good or his clemency will make it so: his graciousness to me will be the same whether he knows me or wills me to be innocent."

And at the end he adds:

"This I have written, as best I could, with a brain decayed and blunted with disuse."

So he closes: but it was not his brain that ailed. Sufficient biographers have expressed their shocked horror. Those who know the awful power of long physical pain to debase, will perhaps be slower to condemn with contempt the victim of the year-long heartache of hopeless banishment.

The philosopher made his great surrender in vain: perhaps it gave Messalina fresh pleasure to see to it that he lost not only the world but now his soul for nothing. Six years longer he was to eat the bitter honey of Corsica. Probably he worked at the pseudo-science with a moral purpose on which he published late in life his *Problems of Natural Science*. Possibly he wrote tragedies. Rome did not forget him: he was read and admired. His popularity was to save him yet—happier perhaps, had he died forgotten in his island banishment!

Now Claudius was so possessed by Messalina that he did not appear to care who else possessed her. But there were limits, not perhaps with the Emperor, but with his freedmen: and when the Empress publicly and religiously married a Roman knight and it looked as if Claudius were on the way to be divorced and deposed by his own wife, they, seeing their own power to depend on his, shook him awake: and before he well knew what had happened, Claudius found himself a widower. The question of a successor to the murdered Messalina tore the Palatine into factions, until Agrippina, niece of Claudius, by her own wits and the support of Pallas carried the day. Her son Domitius was betrothed to Octavia, whose destined husband Silanus committed suicide on Agrippina's wedding-day; her rival Lollia Paulina was hunted to exile and death. To compensate these neither auspicious nor popular commencements of her reign, she bethought her of recalling Seneca.

There were several reasons. He had popularity in Rome, and could confer it with his ready pen: it was like gaining the support of an influential newspaper proprietor, as delicately and as definitely done as might the 20th century. He was a victim of Messalina, her dead enemy, and of her husband Claudius who might yet prove a live one. He had been associated with her sister Julia: whom or at all events whose good name she may well have cared for. He was the very man to educate her young son, to whom her heart, however black, was yet devoted. Lastly scandal, as preserved by Dio Cassius, joined her name, as well as her sister's, with Seneca's.

At all events he was not recalled for nothing; it may well be that he would have preferred a comfortable obscurity and a purely literary fame to further adventures. The Scholiast on Juvenal (v, 109) says he was anxious to go and live at Athens, had not Agrippina detained him, to her undoing and his.

As for him, even philosophers do succumb to flattery judiciously enough applied or implied; perhaps he saw himself treading in Plato's path, with a younger and more tractable prince to be turned into a philosopher, and that with far greater possibilities for human welfare. It is true that Nero's education was rather in humanistic culture than philosophic; his mother would have none of a study she regarded as

unimperial. Nero's own interest in it in later life did not go
beyond the amusement of set dinner-table cock-fights between representatives of the rival sects. Seneca himself,
maliciously adds Suetonius, kept a monopoly of his pupil's
admiration in rhetoric by barring the older orators. A
Satirist on education might dwell on the curious fact that the
worst tyrants of the first and second centuries A.D. were
respectively brought up by their greatest philosophic figures,
Seneca and M. Aurelius. But it is clear that the tutor of
Agrippina's son in the atmosphere of the Palatine had no
easy task; yet one may suspect from the tone of the *Treatise
on Clemency* and from Seneca's own character as one of those
who find it difficult ever to say 'No,' that the boy was
already too much the prince, spoiled and coaxed and flat-
tered. His father had been no mean monster—guilty of
murder and incest; and had remarked at Nero's birth that
the offspring of himself and Agrippina could only be an
abomination and a public danger. And Seneca is said not
only to have dreamed the night after his appointment that
he had become teacher to Caligula, but to have remarked
to his intimates that the young lion in his pupil only needed
to taste human blood to break loose. Apart from this, the
lad was perpetually being pushed into precocious prominence
by his mother, who was engaged in a race for him against
time and Britannicus for the imperial throne.

In 50 Seneca was praetor. In 54 Claudius was poisoned
by his wife, with Nero's knowledge, it is said. With Seneca's
also, after the event, if not before. Burrus the praetorian
prefect was Agrippina's man; the praetorians declared for
Nero; and the Senate acclaimed the inevitable. Nero gave
the watchword "The best of mothers." Seneca's contribution to the occasion, a burlesque of the dead Emperor's
Apotheosis, called the *Pumpkinification of Claudius*, still
survives, unless indeed the extant work is a forgery, which

there is no particular reason to believe it is, however much
ardent admirers of Seneca may want to. For it certainly
provides an illuminating commentary on the high writings
of this voluminous moralist. It would be tedious to give a
detailed outline of this petulantly vicious squib, with its flat
humour and its snarling laughter. Claudius, one "never
properly born even," "bubbles up the ghost" and arrives
at the gate of heaven. Hercules though a connoisseur in
monsters is taken aback at what looks like a thirteenth labour.
The pedantry of Claudius, his trembling hand only steady
enough to order victims to execution, his nonentity in the
eyes of his own freedmen, his passion for sitting in judgment
like Solomon and like Sancho Panza, are all duly sneered at.
After a debate in Heaven he is rejected and escorted through
a Rome rejoicing at the tyrant's death to Hell, where he is
condemned to play with a bottomless dice-box until Caligula
claims him as his slave and he is finally made into an Infernal
lawyer's devil. With this literary horseplay is mixed equally
crude flattery of the seventeen year old Nero as a "young
Apollo golden-haired." One can imagine the scene of the
recitation; the wife who had poisoned her husband, the son
who knew, the moralist who also knew without seeming to
turn one moral hair—these three, and about them the tittering
and guffawing of the great ladies and lords of Rome, laughing
with alien lips like the suitors on their last night in the halls
of Ithaca. It perhaps added slightly to the piquancy of the
situation that Seneca had composed and Nero delivered a
highly polished funeral oration in which not only the birth
and offices and prosperity of the dead Emperor were extolled,
but even his sapience and insight, until the audience burst
out laughing. An instructive lesson in sincerity.

However Seneca, for the next few years, was to be better
than his words; he and Burrus, the blunt, honest soldier,
formed an alliance which only death was to dissolve. Backed

by the power of the sword, though sheathed, Seneca was to
find it easier to make a world happy than his pupil good.
Happier the Empire was for five years, the golden "quin-
quennium Neronis," than at any time in the rest of the
century. So the Emperor Trajan, a weighty witness, judged.

Seneca had the ready brain, Burrus the moral stamina;
their union far more than doubled their strength, as Agrippina
realised to her dismay, when she found her design of using
her new power to make a clean sweep of her enemies confronted by the two men she had herself made. Seneca's
weakness was his love of compromise; it was to prove fatal
with the son; but with the mother even Seneca saw that there
was nothing for it but vigorous resistance. Once he had his
back to the wall, his ready brain had its chance; as when
at the audience of the ambassadors of Armenia, Agrippina
entered the room with the clear design of taking her place
beside the Emperor. Only Seneca had presence of mind to
bid the son rise and go to meet his mother. The audience
was then adjourned, and the danger evaded.

Further, Nero fell in love with a Greek freedwoman, Acte;
Seneca indulged him; it was one blow more at Agrippina's
influence. The empress tried storms, then smiles, equally in
vain; Pallas, her old ally, was dismissed his office; in a new
outburst she threatened to appeal to the army in favour of
Britannicus, the true heir of Claudius, against this usurpation
of the maimed Burrus and the banished Seneca with his
pedant's tongue. The threats of Agrippina were serious; in
reply, shortly afterwards Britannicus fell dead at Caesar's
table. Tacitus distinctly implies that the feeling of men like
Seneca was that such things must happen between rival
claimants to a throne; much as the first-born queen in the
hive kills her yet ungrown sisters.

For the rest Seneca continued bestowing sops upon this
growing Cerberus and happiness on the remainder of man-

kind. He also composed for his pupil his work *On Clemency*; which makes a precarious attempt to render the young autocrat perfect, by telling him that he *is* so. He praises him for maintaining the promise of the first year of his reign; that proves that goodness is his by nature: for "none can long wear a mask!" "You are the mind of the state, the state your body; you see the need for clemency." "Augustus was clement: but his clemency was after all only exhausted savagery." He reminds Nero how, signing one of his early death-warrants, he had groaned "Would I could not write!" The book is eloquent in parts; a lecture on it by Lipsius in after centuries was to confute those who sometimes sneer at Seneca's moralising as completely unconvincing, by moving the Archduke Albert to release three hundred political prisoners; but Nero was probably less edified by the adjurations to mercifulness than inflated by the boundless flattery which emphasises his position as "Regent of the gods on earth and arbiter of the life and death of mankind."

Meanwhile Seneca himself was adding wealth to power; perhaps it was hard in his position not to; but the world at large was not so ready to make allowances for the possessor of £3,000,000, of estates in Italy and abroad, of loans on so vast a scale that their sudden calling in (if the tale be true) could cause a revolt in Britain, and of five hundred identical tables of citron wood with ivory feet. The ever-ready pen might retort in the treatise *On the Happy Life*:

Do you ask why I have more wealth than I can count? I am not yet the perfect wise man, only on the road to perfection; a lame goer, but an Achilles beside you my critic. I despise wealth as much when I have it as when I have it not. My riches belong to me; you belong to yours.

Rome was not altogether convinced.

In 57, Seneca was consul. In 58 Nero was entangled by

Poppaea Sabina, who meant to be empress and cared little
if two lives, Agrippina's and Octavia's stood in the way.
Agrippina was dealt with first (59 A.D.). The fallen empress
was still terrible; when the news arrived that the attempt
made to drown her had miscarried, there was a scene of
dismay in Nero's court at Baiae. He sent for Seneca and
Burrus, whose previous complicity is doubtful; both stood
long silent, says Tacitus, not wishing to use vain dissuasion.
Then Seneca shot a questioning look at Burrus—"Could his
men be ordered to assassinate her?" Bluff as usual, the other
replied that his praetorians could not be trusted against the
daughter of Germanicus. It remained for Anicetus the con-
triver of the fatal ship, to finish his work with the sword;
but it was Seneca's hand that wrote the letter in which Nero
announced and justified his action to the Senate, on the
ground of Agrippina's intolerable and menacing ambition.
There remained little that Nero could do to blacken his own
name; but Seneca's moral acrobatics and supple complaisance
carried to this limit did him no good in men's eyes. It did
not deal "the death-blow to his self-respect" (Mackail)—
nothing ever did that for Seneca—but to his fair fame it must
have done. One phrase of that ill-savoured missive survives:—
"In my own safety I can still neither believe nor rejoice"—
it was echoed till the irony almost shouts, by the orator
Afranius at the head of a congratulatory deputation from
Gaul; "Caesar, your loyal province implores you to bear up
under your good fortune." For three years longer the
coalition of Stoic and soldier kept its power; but Seneca's
policy of trying to quell the conflagration by smothering it
with fuel could only have one end. Nero might for the
moment play the fool rather than the maniac. He might
content himself with being the young Apollo, lord of lyre
and chariot; he might content himself with enacting merely
stage tragedies in his flat and feeble voice, while his old

counsellors sadly applauded, with chanting his poems with
Gallio to proclaim him, Seneca and Burrus to prompt, and
an army of claqueurs specially enrolled. But even had he
been content with the glories of jockey and music-hall artist,
neither Poppaea, now half way to her goal, nor Tigellinus,
the rising favourite, the man who could deprave even Nero,
were so mercifully minded. Burrus when the divorce of
Octavia was broached to him by Nero, merely retorted: "If
you put away the daughter of Claudius, restore her dowry—
the Imperial Throne." Seneca could still repress his pupil's
savagery with the clever platitude: "How ever much blood
you shed, you will never kill your successor." But their power
was doomed. They had compromised, and compromised
themselves; they had glozed three murders and their own
hands were not clean before the world. They had no policy
but resistance to a master growing daily stronger and worse.
Foot by foot they were dragging to the edge. In 62 Burrus
died; poisoned, men said; very probably. Tigellinus filled
his place. A little later Octavia would be exiled and murdered;
and Poppaea would then fill hers. Only this pathetic old man
in his unhappy eminence and gilded misfortune was left; the
opposition yelped louder. How much longer was this
doddering pedant to haunt the Palatine, still grabbing money
(had he not caused Boadicea's rising last year?), still lavishing
it on ostentation, giving himself airs as the one and only
orator, pouring out poetry (perhaps his tragedies) just because
Nero himself had begun to write, carping at the emperor's
driving and the emperor's voice, monopolising the credit of
whatever the Imperial Government did? Nero was old
enough to need no counsellors, but his ancestors. So
Tacitus. Alarmed, like Wolsey, the old man tried jettison.
He sought audience; and with a graceful literary genuflexion
prayed to be allowed to exchange his wealth and eminence
for retirement. The cat with equally velvet delicacy replied

that he could not possibly face the grief and seeming in-
gratitude of parting with this dearly loved mouse. Finally,
Tacitus adds, "as is always the end of conference with
princes," Seneca paid his thanks and took his leave; but he
retrenched and went softly henceforward. He was actually
accused of conspiracy, but unsuccessfully (late 62 A.D.).
Though formal retirement had been refused him, he had
really dropped out of affairs. The last three years of his life
were to be not unhappy; though he had served his prince
better than philosophy, she was not to forsake him in his
grey hairs. He lived with his second wife, young and dearly
loved, who was to go of her own will more than half-way to
death with him; he worked at his *Problems of Natural Science*;
he wrote his *Letters to Lucilius*; he enjoyed his agriculture,—
Columella accords a special mention to his vines; like
Agrippina, he was to be left awhile in peace before the
sudden end.

In 64 Rome was burned and rose in new splendour from
her ashes; but to provide that splendour the offerings and
statues of the gods in Asia and Achaea were ruthlessly
swept away to the Capital. Seneca whose function in the
Imperial eye was no doubt still to provide a certain air of
respectability, rather than bear the responsibility of coun-
tenancing such sacrilege implored to be allowed to rusticate;
forbidden, he confined himself to his room, pleading illness.
A scheme to poison him is said to have miscarried, because
the assassin's nerve failed or because Seneca lived now on
the simplest food, on apples and water.

In 65 came the conspiracy of Piso.

G. Piso of the Calpurnian house, eloquent, open-handed,
affable, with a fine presence and a handsome face, but self-
indulgent and indolent, provided the figure-head. Senators,
knights, officers of the army including Faenius Rufus, joint
praetorian prefect with Tigellinus, enrolled themselves. With

a quarter of the support it won and a little less indecision the conspiracy might well have succeeded. But the most resolute spirits were those with least authority. Epicharis, a freedwoman, chafing at their delay, tried to tamper with a captain in the fleet of Misenum, only concealing the conspirators' names. He at once told Nero; but he had no other evidence and her denials were so resolute, that the Emperor could only keep her under arrest. Subrius Flavus, the tribune, was for stabbing Nero on the stage; it was deemed too dangerous. Then it was suggested that Nero should be killed at Piso's house, where he often stayed, but Piso, apart from less noble reasons of his own, refused to violate hospitality. The day of the Circensian games was at last decided on. But one Scaevinus, who had demanded the leading rôle, by his absurd preparations on the day previous— such as whetting of his sacred dagger, storing of bandages, making his will, giving a last melancholy banquet of forced gaiety—aroused his freedman's suspicion. The freedman had a wife worse than himself. If he did not betray his master, she urged, someone else in the household would; the first to speak would be loaded with rewards; and what good did one man's silence do? He went to Nero. Scaevinus summoned and confronted with his freedman kept his nerve, counter-attacked the man as a vile informer and would have brazened it out, had not the wife remembered that the senator Natalis had been much closeted with her master. When Natalis was sent for and asked on what they had conferred, his story did not tally. At the threat of torture the nerve of both gave way. First Natalis the particular friend of Piso, betrayed that friend's name and also Seneca's; perhaps, says Tacitus, because he had been their go-between, perhaps because he knew Nero would jump at this excuse for murder. Then the betrayals grew like an avalanche, as victim after victim turned informer against his nearest and dearest. Faenius Rufus, not

yet implicated, with the cruelty of the terror-stricken
stormed against his fellow-conspirators; in the very hall of
examination Flavus the tribune, likewise still free, questioned
him with a look "Should he cut down the tyrant then and
there?" His hand was already on his sword-hilt. But Rufus
shook his head; the story is full of the frightful impotence of
a nightmare. Nero was to have three years yet. Only while
the nobility of Rome wilted and cringed, Epicharis the
freedwoman and harlot endured in silence the tortures of
Tigellinus though racked till she could not stand, and
strangled herself at the end by her own breast-band from
her chair.

Rome ran with slaughter; Seneca's time was come; Natalis
said that he had been sent to Seneca to complain of his
refusal to see Piso, and Seneca had replied that it was better
so, but that his life depended on Piso's. Silvanus, a tribune
of the praetorians and himself one of the conspirators, was
despatched to demand an explanation from Seneca, just
returned, not by chance perhaps, from Campania. The
tribune found him dining with his wife and two friends;
Seneca admitted Piso's message but denied his own answer.
What was Piso's safety to him? He was not given to flattering,
as Nero himself knew by experience? Such was the reply
the tribune brought back, where waited that unholy trinity,
Nero, Poppaea and Tigellinus. Their only question was:
"Is he going to kill himself?" The Tribune answered that
there were no signs of it. He was ordered back to break the
brutal truth. On the way he is said to have turned aside to
ask Rufus the guilty prefect if he should obey. But that
broken reed now only knew compliancy. Silvanus went, and
staying without sent in a centurion with the message. The
old man rose to the last occasion of his not inglorious life.
Like Cicero, like Cranmer, men similarly endowed with
more intellect than their will-power could carry, so now

with his back against the wall and no more dilemmas of dreadful indecision, the Stoic was free to be himself. He bade his friends not weep but remember him and their philosophy. His wife insisted on dying with him; with one blow the two severed their veins. But the old man's blood flowed sluggishly; he opened legs and knees as well; the sight of each other's sufferings grew too painful and he persuaded his wife to retire to another room; then he dictated a dying utterance, eloquent to the end. Meanwhile by Nero's orders Paulina's bleeding was stopped; he did not see cause for making himself more odious than necessary; and she lived on some years still, always deathly pale.

Seneca weary of his agony now took some of that poison with which he had long provided himself; the hemlock of Socrates. But his body was too cold for the poison to work. He entered a hot bath sprinkling the slaves and saying, "A libation to Jove the liberator": last of all, he was borne into a vapour bath and suffocated. So ended in perhaps his sixty-ninth year one who had chance been a little different might have died an emperor. For there was said to have been a conspiracy within the conspiracy to send Piso the way of Nero and raise to the purple Seneca instead.

Seneca is not easy to understand, still less to judge. The conventional historian, who probably does not remotely comprehend his own children, assumes a more sublime glibness and intimate familiarity with the characters and motives of the human beings he deals with, the more centuries they have been dead and buried. But it is utter guess-work—realising which let us proceed to guess. What did really lie behind that weary face with its lofty forehead, its weak and high-arched brow, its tired fastidious mouth[1], its look of *laissez-faire*? To begin with the "advocatus diaboli"—Dio Cassius paints in detail a Seneca continually

---

[1] Bust, Berlin Museum, 391.

belying his own preaching, eulogist of liberty and tutor of
a tyrant, a decrier of courtiers who never left the Palatine
himself; condemner of flatterers, yet author of the praises of
Messalina and Claudius' freedman, enemy of riches and
luxury yet possessor of £3,000,000, and of 500 tables of
citron-wood. And he ends his indictment with accusations
of adultery and sexual perversion.

A fierce attack, mostly true; yet how little it all signifies
except a very human inconsistency! It is only because the
majority of mankind are such hypocrites as to take in even
themselves, that they make such a cry about hypocrisy in a
case like this. There are few abominations worse than a conscious hypocrite; but such are far rarer phenomena than is
realised.

Seneca with his high brain-power and the low vitality of
prolonged ill-health, with his clever, subtle mind and his lack
of solid common-sense, with his amiable, but not passionate
temperament, is perhaps after all not so hard to understand.
He desired more than most to do the right thing; but he
hated more than most the unpleasant things, especially
unpleasantness with other people. In a perfectly desperate
position, with only one path before him, he could tread it
finely; but it was a desperate position indeed, when that
agile brain could not find a way round and justify to itself
the same. Less clever he would have proved a great deal
more edifying.

"Je comprends," répondit M. Bergeret, en souriant, "je me
suis toujours incliné à comprendre, et j'y ai perdu des énergies
précieuses. Je découvre sur le tard que c'est une grande force
de ne pas comprendre. Cela permet parfois de conquérir le monde.
Si Napoleon avait été aussi intelligent que Spinoza il aurait écrit
quatre volumes dans une mansarde. Je comprends."

A bright lad, conscious of brains and morally earnest, he
is 'converted'—but not into a fanatic. It is hard for the

really clever to go to the stake; it requires such confidence in one's own opinion. But there exists in every period a creed particularly adapted to men of lively rather than strong intellect and of moral earnestness; in the first century A.D. it called itself Stoicism. A watered and rationalised stoicism, it is true; not that it was ever very rational. The doctrinaire bigotry of a Cato or the beautiful, second-rate mind which looks through the wistful eyes of M. Aurelius might swallow this very wooden camel. But a sceptical Carneades could easily disjoint it and a Horace smother it with genial Epicurean laughter. Seneca's Stoicism had shed its wilder fatuities; he no longer believed that all sins were equal—though the orthodox Stoic view had been that one was either in a state of grace or not; that a handbreadth below the surface one drowned or was damned as completely as a hundred fathoms deep; and that to move one's little finger irrationally was as heinous as choking one's grandmother. He refused to be bound by his predecessors; he could, for heresy is not a word in the vocabulary of philosophy; he sought wisdom even in the enemy's camp among the writings of Epicurus. But the general tone of Stoicism, the cold intellectual Pharisaism, the suppression of emotion as a disease of the intellect, did the innate prig in him no good; and his tragedies are all tinged rather blue by it.

Further asceticism and Schopenhauerianism were ill-fitted for Seneca with his low vitality and his already too negative will. Asceticism, that perverted decadence, is the worst product of luxury. Stoicism was afraid of life, of emotions because they hurt; it could not see that Hell may be worth while, that few Heavens are good enough to enter at the cost of plucking out eyes and shedding limbs. The words of Shaw's Hypatia might have been written for it. "Old, old, old. Squeamish. Can't stand up to things, can't enjoy things. Always on the shrink." Viciously good and morbidly healthy,

the Stoic sage composed himself to float a rigid corpse on
the tide of things; he trained his will that it might will
nothing; he practised an ego-centric altruism. The only
retort to such a view of life is Sir Gringamor's; "As for that
threatening," said Sir Gringamor, "be it as it may, we will
go to our dinner."

However worldly success, bought by concessions, and
worldly failure, which extorts them, must have helped Seneca
to burst some of the straiter Stoic laces. He improved as he
aged. The old gentleman of the letters to Lucilius is really
quite charming. He had had, unluckily for him, few youthful
follies to shed; but, to borrow from Mr Chesterton, he had
at least got rid of some of his youthful wisdom.

One learns a good deal from his writings, taken in judiciously small doses. Quintilian sums him—"not very painstaking in philosophy, but a fine moralist." And a thousand
years after Dante echoes—"Seneca morale." Even in him
the Roman business practicality asserts itself; "minime
mirator inanium" says the Elder Pliny approvingly. He
chafes at the dialectic quibbles of earlier stoics and the
grammatical quibbles of contemporary pedants. What does
it matter about the Homeric question?—Life is not long
enough, even for learning properly to despise life. What is
the use of logical subtleties compared with practical morality?
How shall one resist temptation? "Are you going to face a
lion with a bodkin? Your remarks are indeed pointed. Yet
nothing is more pointed than the spike of a corn-ear; there
are things which their very fineness make useless and
impotent."

It is not a little ironic that this is really the condemnation
of his own moral writings; full of brilliant and subtle
epigrams, which tickle the reader's mind without stirring the
least enthusiasm. His praise of cosmopolitanism ("I was not
born for one corner") of equanimity ("it is a great thing to

have the frailty of man and the tranquillity of God") of
self-realisation ("claim yourself for yourself") and of con-
sistency are all very fine; but when one reads further that
the wise man will not so much mind losing his friends,
because as a skilful Phidias can make new statues, so he
new companions, one is slightly disgusted; when he compares
the converse of the wise to the bites of small creatures, which
are not felt, only their after effects, one is moved to smile;
and when the good man proceeds to relate how his wife has
been trained to lie quiet in bed while he meditates on his
actions during the day, there is nothing for it but profane
laughter. Once more it may be magnificent to demonstrate
that it is as noble for the rich man to use gold plate as if it were
earthenware as it is for the poor man to use earthenware as
if it were gold; still it does not quite cover that £3,000,000.

Yet if he was sometimes a little worse than his creed, he
was sometimes better. In spite of his unpleasant theory of
friendship, he mourned so bitterly for Annaeus Severus, that
he became a bye-word; he apologises for it; had he but
known how needlessly! But, apart from their Stoicism, his
philosophic works throw a certain amount of light on the
man himself. If a prig, he is a good-hearted prig. He lifts
a solitary voice of protest at the gladiatorial shows—a faint
forerunner of St Telemachus. "Man, who should be sacred
to man, is slaughtered now in play and jest." But, rather
surprisingly, our Stoic is no prohibitionist of humaner things;
of wine he says: "Sometimes one may go even to the point
of getting drunk—only so far, however, as to be just sub-
merged not drowned." And one sees how the amiability
begins to fade into weakness in utterances like "never
withstand the angry" and his half approving quotation of
the words of the Old Courtier who, being asked the secret
of his successful career, replied "Taking kicks and saying
'Thank you.'"

In the work of his fallen old age, the most attractive of all his writings, the *Letters*, there are no allusions to his own past greatness, but bitterly disillusioned aphorisms on greatness in general, to the powerful of the moment "trembling on the summit of envied eminence," "tortured by their high place, in enjoyment of their own curse." There is a similarly bitter allusion in the earlier treatise *On Tranquillity* to the other side of greatness, its parasites—"rushing as though to a fire—they dash into everyone in their path and trip up themselves and others in their haste; and yet all this helter-skelter is only to pay a salutation to someone who will not return it, or to follow the funeral of someone they do not know."

For he has the wit, if only occasionally the will, to be mordant. Of Marcellinus, a common acquaintance, he writes to Lucilius: "He visits us seldom, only because he is afraid of hearing some hometruth; he is past that danger now." He delivers a passing thrust at the ritualists of his day. "Let us have no kindling of candles on the Sabbath; the Gods do not need light, and even men take no delight in soot"; and at the busy business-man, "He thinks he has friends, though he is friend to none." He is a humorist too in a modest way, as when he parodies contemporary exquisites with the story of Snimdirides of Sybaris who was exhausted by seeing a labourer dig and blistered behind by sitting on a crumpled roseleaf; and when he remarks of the custom of keeping pet fools, "Personally, I find myself sufficient."

As for literary style, if he chose the worse, it was not apparently for want of knowing the better; he praises particularly the manner of Fabianus "whose style followed him as naturally as his shadow"—and he commends elsewhere the utterance "of self-reliance rather than elaboration."

And even his own, in the moments when his sincerity rings clear, ceases in Fronto's bitter phrase "to mouthe," and becomes really eloquent with a note not unbecoming one whose name the Middle Ages linked with St Paul's. We may quote a few fragments here.

On Virtue, the highest good.

How, say you, shall I come thither? Not across the Pennine or the Graian Alps; not across the deserts of Candavia. You need not near the Syrtes, nor Scylla nor Charybdis; though past all these you, my Lucilius, have journeyed for the sake of petty office. This road is safe, is pleasant; the road for which Nature has prepared you. She has given you that, which if you hold fast, you shall rise to equal God. But equal to God money will not make you; God has nought. Purple will not make you; God is naked. Glory will not make you, nor pomp and pride, nor your name spread abroad throughout the world; for no man knows God, and many think ill of Him, unpunished. Nor yet will a crowd of servants bearing your litter through Roman streets and roads abroad, equal you to Him; for God the All-highest and Almighty Himself bears all.

On Mortality.

Say to me before I sleep, "You may not wake." Say when I awake, "You may never sleep again." Say as I go forth, "You may not return." Say when I return, "You may never go forth more."

On the Golden Age of Rousseau—the Noble Savage.

No panelled ceilings hung above them; but as they lay in the open the stars glided overhead and the radiant splendour of the night; headlong swept the firmament, wheeling its mighty fabric silently.

On Liberty.

Wherever you turn, there is the end of ills. Do you see that precipice? There is the descent to liberty. Do you see that ocean, that river, that well? At its bottom sits liberty. Do you see that tree, stunted, blasted, barren? There hangs liberty. Do you see your neck, your throat, your breast? They are refuges from servitude. Do you ask which is the road to liberty? The least vein in your body.

It is all purple; but not bad, as purple goes.

To conclude, his life was marred because he did not know how to make—in the opposite to Dante's sense—"great refusals." Like a once outstanding figure of our own day, also a master of words and for a little while almost master of the world, Seneca failed because he never saw when he must fling compromise to the winds[1].

However, the rule which gave civilised mankind for nearly seven years peace and quiet in which to be happy if they could, was, if a failure, after all considerably above most human successes. Seneca like "Madame de Mouchy," like most of us, was indeed better than his life.

They have much wisdom, yet they are not wise;
  They have much goodness, but they do not well;
They have much strength, but still their doom is stronger;
Much patience, but their time endureth longer;
  Much valour, but life mocks it with some spell[2].

[1] See J. M. Keynes, *Economic Consequences of the Peace*, ch. III.
[2] J. Thomson, *City of Dreadful Night*.

CHAPTER III

THE TRAGEDIES OF SENECA

To understand the atmosphere, the time and the public of Seneca the tragedian, we must take up the thread where we left it, at the fall of the Republic.

The Empire was a new world. Rome the city was becoming ever less, the Provinces ever more. All through the first centuries A.D. the capital is sinking step by step to a mere municipality; that process is as yet only beginning; but there is already a new Cosmopolitanism; the Syrian Orontes, as Juvenal wails, is pouring into the Tiber, the distinctively Roman tone of Roman literature is gone. The Romanised provincial slowly provincialises Rome. And so in Seneca himself, the critics have traced the egotism of the hidalgo of Castile, the macabre rant, the melodramatic cruelty of the land of bullfights and Lope de Vega. Much of this may well be fanciful; but that Roman literature with all this influx of exotics should become less classical was inevitable; and it becomes comprehensible too that the France and Spain and England of the Renaissance should have found in the tragedies of a Spaniard, written for an already provincialised Rome, something far nearer akin to them and theirs than the pure and classic splendours, the white radiance of the Attic Stage.

But secondly it was not merely this literary invasion of the barbarians that made Silver Latin less classical; it was also the mere fact that it followed the supremely classical Golden Age of the Augustans. They had said so much and said it so well, that their posterity found themselves faced with the dilemma of saying *consciously* the same as they had or saying *consciously* something different. Imitation is poor inspiration and means dullness; being different for the sake of being different, is demoralising and means extravagance. The Imperial writers became either melodramatically wild like Lucan or ultra-classically tame like Statius; just as Chinese poetry became swamped with its own classical tradition. Seneca with his restrained diction and avoidance of mouth-filling sonority, but also his *outré* epigrams and his emotional hyperboles, suffers from both maladies at once.

But, for these reasons too, the Renaissance, with its wits preternaturally stimulated and with its emotions, while still full of Medieval Romanticism, now new-kindled by the old wine of Greece and Rome, found in him its Tragic Poet.

Thirdly, the Empire had not only brought the Provinces into their own and Roman culture to its climax; it had given Rome peace, but only at the price of liberty, it had given men time for literature only at the price of life. That is, it had given only to take away.

"He that would not be frustrated," says Milton, "of his hope to write well hereafter, ought himself to be a true poem." That is where the academic always fails. Now, one of the vividest things in Roman life had been oratory. Latin, that magnificently sounding tongue, had naturally the vigour, and had acquired the polish, to be one of the most splendid instruments eloquence has ever wielded. It had become so, because it was bound up with the very life of Republican Rome. In the Senate and the Law-courts, before the Roman People, the man who would reach power must have the gift of weighty speech. The great trials were themselves political. By words alone Cicero had raised himself from the municipal obscurity of hill-girt Arpinum to the highest offices in Rome.

Then came the Empire; the ghosts of the Republic were carefully preserved. Elections and debates were still held with all pomp and circumstance. But all was empty show.

In the Senate, one word from Caesar outweighed a hundred perorations; even the eloquence of the law-courts decayed; for the popular juries had been largely replaced by the court of the centumviri, who were more concerned with the law and less with rhetoric. Only the schools flourished; and if men still devoted themselves with impassioned ardour to deliberating in the person of Agamemnon, whether to sacrifice or not to sacrifice Iphigeneia, yet, since they were really concerned not to express a man ten centuries buried, but to impress the fashionable audience sitting there all ears before them, they inevitably cared more and more for brilliance and less and less for sense. Hence that style where, as Quintilian says, "little was brilliant, but everything was said as if it were." Hence the waste of words which engulfed the thought of the Empire. Men had ceased to have new things to say, or new words to say them in; nothing was left but to polish the old phrases and grind the old points to tawdry glitter and niggling sharpness. Men were still discussing the same fatuous imaginary cases (for instance, is a son bound to support a father who has refused to redeem him from the pirates?) in the days of Ennodius in the fifth century, when the last fabric of the Western Empire was tottering about their ears.

Hence comes the exasperatingly false rhetoric of the Senecan stage, with its far-fetched and frigid epigrams; hence the delight of the Elizabethan, loving gorgeous declamation, and doting on 'conceits,' in this newly reopened mine of flashy phrase.

Fourthly, not only the writer, but his public also suffered from the political stagnation of the time. They too had lost touch with reality; politics and patriotism were either dull or dangerous. Philosophy was shorn and narrowed. They had to be stung awake by novelty, and not bored by anything too deep. The reading public was an upper class clique, with a classical education; thence the pedantry and sackfuls of learned allusion in the works of the time.

This last evil was aggravated owing to the practice intro-duced by Asinius Pollio of public recitation of literary works—a poor substitute for the old freedom of speech. Success under these conditions became a matter of short purple patches, not of the artistic construction of an *Iliad.* The craze for epigram, the fear of anything profound or delicate was doubly potent, when literature became a means of killing afternoons for fashionable audiences. One begins to realise why Seneca developed that style, the continued reading of which an irritated Macaulay likened to "dining off anchovy sauce." His tragedies were not acted, though the Renaissance thought so and acted them; they were recited. To forget that is to misunderstand thĕm from the start—they are really chamber-drama.

The result of this recitation is that Senecan drama tends to be an alternation of melancholy monologues and epigram-matic duologues with musical interludes by the chorus between the now established five acts. In a recited play it is a strain on the powers of the reciter and on the imagination of the audience, to have a dialogue which is more than a duologue. Senecan plays in general observe the Attic con-vention of not having more than three speaking actors, apart from the Chorus, simultaneously upon the stage; but in practice they can seldom manage more than two and a half.

Next, the characters of the recited play tend to talk all in the same way. I do not say—if one may use the metaphor—that Seneca, had he had the real dramatic instinct, might not have ventriloquised well enough for his puppets' utter-ances to sound quite individual and distinct. But Seneca with his egotistic Stoicism, even had he written ordinary acting plays, would have found it hard enough to animate and individualise his characters; and in pieces meant only for reading or recitation the temptation to make all his creatures talk the same clever rant becomes overwhelming.

Again, since the play is not acted, it tends to have less and less action, and the whole burden is thrown upon the language. Seneca's audience was steeped in rhetoric and in the Augustan poets. Therefore that language had to be violently rhetorical, whether in set speeches, or in cut-and-thrust stichomuthia, and it had to be variegated with purple patches of description and allusion to those Augustans in the super-fine poetic style.

But here also was a source of its influence on a Tudor England just realising of what oratorical magnificence its own English tongue was capable, an England intellectually young and therefore delighting in truth thrown about like squibs, an England, too, intellectually raw and crude and therefore loving the lurid extravagances of Senecan bombast and flamboyance.

The absence of action had another result. In Greek tragedy horrors abounded, but they were kept off the stage; Horace's remark is hackneyed: "Let not Medea kill her children before the audience." In Senecan tragedy, as there is no real stage, the horrors are sometimes part of the action, not always as in the Attic dramatists related by a messenger, or only heard, not seen. Thus Hercules' murder of his children, if not actually imagined as taking place on the stage, is described, as it happens, by one who sees it from the stage; and the dismembered pieces of the body of Hippolytus are brought on and fitted together, jigsaw-like, by his father, who complains in the usual smooth iambics of the difficulty of knowing which is which.

The reason for this change is to be sought not only in the greater natural brutality of the Roman mind, which could gloat over mimes where a criminal in the part of Laureolus was crucified and torn by a bear, or in the part of Hercules

on Oeta burned alive; if only to make up for the unreality
of this ultra-academic drama the author tries to be vivid by
being lurid, to stimulate the jaded imagination of his public
by screaming atrocity. Seneca does indeed recall the man in
Plato, who had a morbid desire to view the corpses in the
city-ditch; long ashamed to yield to such an impulse, at last
he ran to the edge and uncovered his eyes, with the cry,
"There, you wretches, take your fill."

Here, too, the Elizabethan followed, with a difference; not
only did the cock-fighting, bear-baiting audiences of South-
wark like plenty of blood and thunder, and therefore insist
on representing actually on the stage, whatever Seneca had
left to the imagination; but even the academic playwrights
of the Universities, taking for granted that Seneca had been
staged and acted in Rome, staged and acted even worse than
Senecan horrors at Oxford and Cambridge. In 1592 Alabaster's *Roxana* was performed at Trinity College, Cambridge,
a typical Senecan imitation, which ends in a cannibal orgy
of revenge so ghastly, that a gentlewoman in the audience
"fell distracted and never recovered." Similarly, on the
popular stage in that play of *King Cambises* destined to
become a by-word for rant, one Sisamnes was actually flayed
alive with a false skin before the public eye.

Finally, an obvious result of writing merely literary plays
was that actual dramatic effect was neglected. Seneca might
have answered in that haughty phrase "that he knew his art,
not his trade": but as Ward points out, it would have seemed
a poor answer to the genuine Elizabethan. It was there that
the practical Renaissance playwright soon bettered his
instruction. Seneca had almost everything, talent, culture,
style, a great and sonorous language, a magnificent literary
ancestry, a divine tradition to follow and maintain; but a
living soul he had not. That is always the damnation and
second death of literary coteries and artistic cliques that creep

away from the world to whisper to each other of art for art's sake in holes and corners. It was just this crude and effervescent vigour and vitality of a newly awakened populace, of a nation that had found itself, that enabled the Elizabethans to put the breath of life into these dead bones of the Latin Decadence, which had indeed not ever properly lived before. And yet, even so, let us not forget the debt we do owe to the fashioner of these bones, of the skeleton-framework to which Marlowe and Shakespeare were to give flesh and blood and life.

To summarise then the influences of the time; in general, an ever more cosmopolitan Rome provincialised the best classical style, the almost tyrannical tradition of the Augustans made writers who conformed to it ultra-classic and those who rebelled melodramatically romantic, the political stagnation of autocracy forced authors and public alike to become dilettante and academic, craving to feed their jaded appetites on fustian rhetoric and orgies of epigram; next, in drama in particular, the substitution of recited for acted plays developed more and more the purple patch, the mere tawdry brilliance of language, the habit of kicking an audience awake with horror piled on horror, while true dramatic effect and characterisation were neglected; lastly, in Seneca himself, Stoicism induced an egotistic hardness, a wooden uniformity in his characters, and a substitution of hysterical sentiment for emotion, which removes him whole worlds from his master Euripides.

For the Stoic, however altruistic, remained an egotist. It is misleading to write like M. Waltz, one of Seneca's most recent biographers—"Il n'aime pas de parler de lui-même—il préfère les lieux communs. On dirait que le moi lui paraît haïssable, jusque dans le moi du prochain." This forgets the insistent Stoic "Vindica te tibi." It is not his 'ego' that the Stoic hates, it is the emotions that make personality. Seneca cares about this 'ego' extremely, but it is a bottle-imp, glass-walled, mopping and mowing in a colourless void, hermetically sealed from the dust and colour of life. Only because that self is so maimed and docked, because he has severed hands and plucked out eyes to enter this bottled paradise, his individuality is so colourless and unapparent, like a live shrimp, that it may be overlooked and mistaken for impersonality. But really the Stoic is a lofty egotist, preserving himself in ice; such temperaments may be moral, they are hardly poetic.

It is worth contrasting Keats' account of the poet's soul.

It is not itself—it has no self. It is everything and nothing. It lives in gusto, be it foul or fair, high or low, rich or poor, mean or elevated. It has as much delight in conceiving an Iago as an Imogen. A poet is the most unpoetical of anything in existence, because he has no identity; he is continually in, and filling some other body.

And elsewhere—

The setting sun will always set me to rights; or if a sparrow come before my window, I take part in its existence, and pick about the gravel.

This may be exaggerated; such a theory will not find room for a Byron. But its considerable truth emphasises the difficulty of a Stoic Seneca becoming a real poet, above all a dramatic one. There must always be an antipathy between the poetic and the philosophic mind. It is ill enough when philosophers gird at poetry: but when they try to write it!

The Stoic then had banned emotion; and when he wants to stage it, he can only produce hysteria. Euripides has been compared in his intellectualism to a lion who has to lash himself to fury with his own tail; Seneca, in a far more artificial age and with a far more artificial creed, has to flog himself with his, to attain his high fantastic frenzies.

It remains to illustrate these tendencies from the plays themselves. These are ten in number; the *Octavia* and the

Hercules Oetaeus, at least the bulk of it, are not by Seneca. The *Phoenissae* is a fragment. The authenticity of the *Agamemnon* has been questioned. There remain the *Hercules Furens*, the *Troades*, the *Medea*, the *Phaedra* based on Euripides; the *Oedipus*, on Sophocles; and the *Thyestes*.

First then, our Spaniard has lost all that is best in classicism, the restraint, the sense of proportion, of due measure, of "nothing too much." "Everything too much" is the keynote of his work: his very virtues, his cleverness, his gift of expression, are exaggerated to a fault. The Greek of the great period, as Sidney Irwin points out, never "confounds his skill in covetousness"—he has that supreme gift, the knowledge what to leave unsaid. And typical is Homer's story of the meeting of Odysseus' comrades with the Queen of the Laestrygones.

> She was tall as a mountain and they abhorred her.

She offended their sense of proportion. Now all Seneca's characters are perpetually straining to be as tall as mountains until they prick themselves on the points of their own epigrams and collapse like wind-blown bladders, or burst, like the fabulous frog, with their own tumidity.

His tyrants for instance far out-Herod any Creon or Lycus of Greek tragedy. The Atreus of his *Thyestes* is a criminal maniac: and the play rather mental pathology than drama. The plot is as simple as revolting; Thyestes has seduced the wife of Atreus and tried to usurp his throne; Atreus in return feeds him on the flesh of his own children. In Act I Atreus appears plotting vengeance.

> Fall now this mighty house of famous Pelops,
> And crush me, so it crush my brother too.
> Come dare, my heart, a crime no age shall pardon,
> But no age e'er forget. Venture some deed
> Bloody and fell, such as my brother would
> Wish to be *his*. Nothing avenges crimes
> But what surpasses them.   (*Thyestes* 190–6.)

And again

> Ubicumque tantum honesta dominanti licent
> Precario regnatur.   (214–15.)

> "That ruler who dares only do what's *right*
> Rules but on sufferance."

One of the usual Senecan puppet-counsellors, after feeble remonstrance, acquiesces in this plan of vengeance on Thyestes.

> Ferro peremptus spiritum inimicum expuat.   (245.)

> "Slain by the sword
> Let him spew out the life thou hatest so."

But Atreus replies

> De fine poenae loqueris: ego poenam volo.
> Perimat tyrannus lenis: in regno meo
> Mors impetratur.   (246–8.)

> "Nay that's release from pain: 'tis pain I want.
> Kind is the king that kills: in my kingdom
> Death is a boon."

The Messenger relates how Atreus killed and dismembered the children of Thyestes; straightway the sun hid his face, the earth quaked, the votive wine turned to blood. Only the tyrant is still himself.

> Movere cunctos monstra, sed solus sibi
> Immotus Atreus constat atque ultro deos
> Terret minantes.   (703–5.)

> "All quailed before those horrors: only Atreus
> Stood constant and unmoved, yea terrified
> The threatening Gods themselves."

Lastly, watching his victim at his unconscious cannibal feast, he makes the crowning utterance

> Eructat. O me caelitum excelsissimum
> Regumque regem. Vota transcendi mea.   (911–2.)

> "Look, now he belches! God of Gods am I,
> And King of Kings; I have surpassed my prayers."

Such is the Senecan tyrant, ancestor of a poisonous progeny. But it is not only his tyrants; everyone and everything is limned in the same crude oleograph colours, with the same melodramatic exaggeration. His heroes are megalomaniacs, his virgins viragos; his very infants die with the callousness of Stoic philosophers. His Hercules is a gladiator; his Oedipus a Bedlamite. Courage in him becomes suicidal mania; fortitude a perverse lust for torture. He cannot poison a woman without a pharmacopoeia; he cannot raise a ghost without letting loose all the damned souls in Hell.

But as a *reductio ad nauseam* of the whole tasteless barbarism the Messenger's story of the self-blinding of Oedipus will serve.

> A sudden storm of tears burst o'er his face,
> Flooded his cheeks. "Are tears enough?" he cried.
> "Only so gently shall mine eyes rain down?
> Torn from their sockets they shall follow forth
> Their tears; does that suffice, ye gods of wedlock?
> Out with my eyes!" He spoke, and raved in fury:
> His threatening visage blazed with a savage fire,
> His eyes scarce held themselves within their sockets,
> Fearless and fell his face,—maddened with rage,—
> One burst of frenzy. He groaned and with a cry
> Laid hands upon his face. To meet his hands
> His glaring eyes stood out and straining followed
> Of their own will the grasp that tore them free,
> Running to meet their ravisher. Greedily
> He groped with his hooked fingers for their orbs
> And from the inmost socket dragged and wrenched
> Both eyeballs loose at once....   (*Oed.* 953–69.)

So it goes on: but we, thank Heaven, need not. The revolting sufficiently intensified becomes the ludicrous. When one savours lines like:

> Terribile dirum pestilens atrox ferum;
> "Terrible, dire, pestilent, ferocious, grim";

when, as Hercules murders his children, one of them is announced to have died of fright before the club brained it, when in the *Oedipus*, at the ghost-raising of Tiresias the leaves of the trees stand on end and their bark cracks with horror, the reader either laughs or yawns. It is all too like the savage adorning his Mumbo-Jumbo with grinning teeth and goggly eyes, till his god becomes a golliwog. Nor is it only the bad taste of exaggeration that fixes so great a gulf between Seneca and the truly classic; the bad taste of over-cleverness, as well as of over-emphasis, the craze for frigid conceits as well as for rant and bluster, are everywhere. Well for the English stage, had the Elizabethan lapped up both a little less eagerly.

Thus when Hercules goes to Hell, the ghosts of the monsters are panic-stricken; the wraith of the Hydra hides its hundred diminished heads in the furthest corner of the Stygian marsh; and the intimidated Cerberus actually wags his snaky tail. In another of the numerous Infernos of our author, the proud Niobe numbers her fourteen spectre-children—as now she safely can—for no jealous gods can kill their ghosts. Andromache hears that her little son lies mangled where he was flung from the last tower of Troy; she forgets grief in repartee. "Another likeness to his father"—she retorts—to the mangled Hector, that is, dragged at Achilles' chariot-wheels. Polyxena sacrificed at Achilles' tomb, flings herself down hard and angrily in death, as if to make the ground lie more heavily upon her destroyer. Oedipus finds his sorrows' crown of sorrow in his inability, now that he has put out his eyes, even to weep!

And lastly, listen to that same ingenious soul's summary of his tangled relationships.

His grandsire's son-in-law, his father's rival,
His children's brother and his brother's sire.
At one same birth his grandmother brought forth
Sons for her husband, grandsons for herself.   (*Phoen.* 134-7.)

Even Thyestes, having swallowed his children, checks himself, beating his breast, with the sublime fatuity,

> Parcamus umbris.
> "Let us spare the buried dead."

Always the same heartless, devilish, devastating cleverness.

On the other hand, apart from these anti-classical extravagances, the ultra-classical side of the Silver Age has equally left its mark upon his work. That excessive smoothing of the metre and avoidance of elision which makes the Silver Latin Epic poets so sickly and emasculate after the Virgilian hexameter, conventionality in dramatic structure, in the types of character, tyrants each with his counsellor, heroines each with her nurse, stock deities, stock mythology—all the chineseries of an ossified culture are his. Once the Labours of Hercules are mentioned, the reader knows he must himself toil through the whole dreary list; once the tortures in Hell of Tantalus or Tityus are alluded to, one knows that Seneca is going in a line or two, with the inexorable regularity of a machine, to grind out more of his infinite variations on the companion tortures of Ixion and Sisyphus. Never, never does one of these gentry appear—and appear they do with maddening frequency—but one knows the other three inseparables are imminent.

Next there is Seneca's rhetoric; no other one word sums up the whole nature of the plays so completely. Their faults, their virtues, their exaggerations, their bad taste, their vigour and their point are all rhetorical. It must indeed be owned that the set speeches do sometimes rise to real eloquence, for instance Agamemnon's in the *Troades*. He is opposing the demand of Pyrrhus, son of Achilles, that Polyxena, daughter of Priam, shall be sacrificed on Achilles' tomb.

> Youth ever fails to curb its own hot blood,
> But what in others is but youthful heat,

In Pyrrhus is his father's headiness.
Patient long since I bore with the fierce spirit,
And threats of proud Achilles. 'Tis e'en so:
With greatest power should greatest patience go.
   But why now stain a noble warrior's shade
With murder? Nay, thou must learn first of all
What conquerors may inflict, and conquered suffer.
A violent power no ruler wields for long,
A moderate lasts and lives. The loftier
Fortune exalts and lifts the might of man,
The lowlier should her favourite bear himself
And fear the change of chance and dread the gods,
Too kindly grown. That greatness in a moment
Falls, I have learnt by conquest. What! does Troy
Make *us* now proud and wanton? We Greeks stand,
There where she fell. I do confess, *sometimes*
I have in pride of power dealt haughtily:
But all that arrogance is cured in me,
By what in others breeds it,—Fortune's favour.
'Tis thou, dead Priam, that makest me at once
Both proud and fearful. Can I believe my power
More than an empty glittering name, a false
Circlet about my brows? Swift chance will snatch
All this away nor need a thousand ships
Nor ten years' war, maybe. Ah not on all
So slowly do the threats of Fortune fall.

                                        (*Troades* 250–78.)

Great too are the indignant defence of the betrayed Medea,
and the speech where Phaedra declares to Hippolytus her
love for the face the youthful Theseus wore in old days,
which now lives again in him, the invective of Clytemnestra
in the *Agamemnon* against the war-lord who has waged ten
years of war and sacked a city to punish adultery, an adulterer
himself, the callous autocrat who could sacrifice a daughter
so readily, though he would not sacrifice a concubine, in his
people's—or his own ambition's—cause.

The gorgeous oratory of the Elizabethan stage, the splen-

dours of a *Hamlet* and a *Julius Caesar* were to owe no small
debt even to these utterances of degenerate Rome.

Similarly, scattered here and there in the tragedies, certain
isolated phrases, in spite of the instinctive English squirming
at the rhetorical, which still makes much even of a play like
Cyrano de Bergerac seem to us odd and high falutin' and
foreign, in spite too of the reader's persistent feeling that
Seneca is, in his own words "withstanding a lion with a
bodkin," in his efforts to cope with the tragic by means of
the merely ingenious—certain phrases do thrust home and
bite. Such are Clytemnestra's taunt of the womanish
Aegisthus:

> Adultery his manhood's only proof,   (*Agam.* 299.)

the curse of the house of Atreus:

> Foully let all its sons be slain—
> And yet more foully born,   (*Thyestes* 41–2.)

the curse of Medea on Jason—let him have

> The bitterest curse that I can pray for him,
> Sons like their sire, and like to me, their mother,
>   (*Medea* 24–5.)

and the cry of Hercules, when he wakes to find he has
murdered his own children and feels that only self-slaughter
can wipe out his guilt.

> If I live, I've sinned: if I die, I was sinned against.
>   (*Hercules Furens* 1278.)

These things in the sheer force of their scorn, their anger or
their agony have a genuine touch of greatness.

Equally characteristic is the Senecan Stichomuthia or line
for line repartee, offspring of the Euripidean, but polished
and sharpened to thrust and parry like a rapier, to stab like
a stiletto. Perhaps the finest of all these verbal fencing-
matches is the passage in the *Troades* (322–48) between
Pyrrhus and Agamemnon; but there is a typical duel between
Megara, wife of Hercules, who has gone to Hades to fetch at

Eurystheus' bidding the dog Cerberus, and Lycus usurper
of Thebes, who is trying to force her to wed him.

Lycus.   Art thou so proud of a husband lost in Hell?
Megara. He entered Hell, that he might scale the Heavens.
Lyc. Well, now he's crushed beneath the massive earth.
Meg. The back that bore the sky *no* load can crush.
Lyc. I'll force thee. *Meg.* None is forced that dares to die.
Lyc. Nay, tell me, what royal gift shall I prepare
     To grace our bridals? *Meg.* Thy death or mine own.
Lyc. Fool, thou shalt die. *Meg.* So I shall meet my lord.
Lyc. Dost prize a slave above our royal crown?
Meg. How many kings that "slave" has sped to death!
Lyc. Then why serves he a king, and bears a yoke?
Meg. Remove all harsh commands: and what is virtue?
(Hercules Furens 422–33.)

Unfortunately here too Seneca never knew where to stop:
only too often this bandying of alternate epigrams, by the
dozen smacks more of a comic ale-house than a tragedy. Yet
by themselves some of his retorts have a real magnificence.

A typical nurse is dissuading the deserted Medea from
vengeance:

Nurse.   Colchis is far, thou canst not trust thy lord,
     Of all thy power nothing is left to thee.
Medea. Medea is left![1]   (*Medea* 164–6.)

Again, the feeble Jason remonstrates with the angry wife who
has stained her soul with a father's betrayal and a brother's
murder, all for love of him.

Jason.   But still what crime canst thou impute to me?
Medea. All those that I have done.   (*Medea* 497–8.)

Lastly, at the close of the *Thyestes*,—a scene hollow with
the cackling laughter of fiends, heavy with something like
the sickly, poisonous atmosphere of Poe's *Cask of Amon-*

---

[1] Cf. Corneille's *Médée*:
    " Dans un si grand revers, que vous reste-t-il?—Moi!
    Moi, dis-je, et c'est assez!"

tillado, Atreus reveals to his brother, the seducer of his wife, that he has been feasted on his children's flesh; and the trapped Thyestes screams:

> Ah, why should my sons suffer? *Atreus.* For being thine.
> *Thy.* A Sire on his son's flesh! *At.* Ay and, glad thought,
> No bastards *they. Thy.* Hear me, O righteous Gods!
> *At.* The gods of wedlock?   (*Thyestes* 1100–3.)

And then the mocker flings at his wife's paramour the last and bitterest jeer. "Are you thus wild with grief" he sneers, "because you have eaten your own children? No, but because you have been outstripped, because you have lost the chance of feeding me on mine."

> Only one thing deterred you—
> You thought my sons were yours!
>   (*Thyestes* 1110.)

The third manifestation of the rhetorician in Seneca, besides his set harangues and his gladiatorial duels of repartee, is the eternal epigram, the jewels, too often only paste, of the compiler of commonplaces, the sententious quotations which a Kyd or a Marston loved to set, still in their native Latin, amid his own blank verse, like strange exotic blooms in an English garden. One might make a small anthology on tyranny alone.

> When a king hates, he makes guilt, seeks it not.
>   (*Agam.* 280.)

> He fain would do what he should not do,
> Who can do what he will.   (*Phaedra* 215.)

> They lust to be feared, to be feared they dread,
> No kindly night in security
> Pillows the anxious monarch's head,
> His heart from care no slumbers free.   (*Agam.* 73–6.)

So Atreus sneers when his counsellors dissuade him from letting his sons share his cannibal vengeance, lest their young hearts should be corrupted:

> Why, though none teach them treachery and crime
> Royalty will do it. Thou fearest they'll grow bad.
> Princes are born *that*.   (*Thyestes* 312-4.)

So of birth and death, God and man, epigrams, ever epigrams.

Of the security of death, the sure refuge.

> None is too weak to rob a man of life,
> None strong enough to rob a man of death.
>
> > (*Phoen.* 152-3.)

Of the gods. Theseus finds he has murdered his innocent Hippolytus and cries in vain in his remorse to Heaven:

> The gods heed not my prayers:
> Did I but ask them crimes, how ready they!
>
> > (*Phaedra* 1242-3.)

Of prodigies:

> That man fears omens, who has nought worse to fear.
>
> > (*Troades* 610.)

We have already traced the effect of writing for recitation before jaded audiences, in the manufacture of purple patches to keep them awake and in the exploitation of horrors and flesh-creepiness worthy the fat boy in *Pickwick* to prevent them from going to sleep.

Examples of such patches are the hurricane which wrecks the Greek fleet in the *Agamemnon*, the devil-raising of Tiresias in the *Oedipus*, that most irrelevant Inferno as described by Theseus in the *Hercules*, the account of the slaying of Hippolytus by the sea-bull in the *Phaedra*, the stories of the ends of Astyanax and Polyxena in the *Troades*. They are always violent, sometimes vigorous, occasionally fine; they would be finer, were there less fine writing about them all. But a certain verve they have.

As for the horrors, mostly in the vein of Mme Tussaud, we need not dwell on them ourselves. One example will probably more than suffice. At the end of the *Phaedra* the fragments of Hippolytus are brought in, and the Chorus and his father Theseus, address themselves lugubriously to making an attempt to put him together again. But alas, their efforts are in vain as those of the king's horses and the king's men to do the like service for Humpty-Dumpty.

The Chorus begins:

> The scattered members of his mangled frame,
> O Father, set in order, and restore
> To their true place his errant limbs: see here
> His right hand goes, and here his left, so skilled
> To hold the reins: I recognize the mark
> Of his left side. How large a part, alas,
> Remains yet lost and absent from our tears.

Theseus continues:

> O trembling hands endure your mournful office,
> O cheeks be dry and stay your flood of tears,
> While this poor father numbers his son's limbs,
> And forms his body. What thing is this so shapeless,
> And so befouled,—torn, mangled every side?
> Which part of thee, I doubt: but some part, sure;
> Well, lay it here, not where it should belong,
> But where there's room.   (*Phaedra* 1256–68.)

Of philosophy, in any real sense, little is to be found in our plays—though there are philosophic tags in plenty and abundance of moralising; and the would-be sympathetic characters have all the wooden inhumanity of genuine Stoics. But there is none of the intense feeling, however pessimistic, about the world and life, which makes an Aeschylus, a Euripides, or a Thomas Hardy, none of that passion for living at all and any cost, which sometimes will not let one sleep at nights, and which redeems and uplifts the very adages and aphorisms of the Elizabethan from the stuffy pettinesses of the Senecan conventicle to the shouting of youth and the winds of morning across a world dewy and expectant in the hushed grey of a new dawn.

The only philosophic note in Seneca which really rings true is one, which however inconsistent with his own creed—for it is frankly and surprisingly Epicurean—is far more in harmony with the only honest human feeling about life such an age could really have. In the famous Chorus of the *Troades* on Death, in the praise of sleep in the *Hercules*, "of human life the better part," in the pessimism and weariness which falls sometimes like a blessed quiet across the shriekings and stridencies of Seneca's usual *fortissimo*—in all these one feels that the true spirit of the Rome, though not the Empire, of the first century A.D. is finding a momentary expression, an anticipation of the magnificent despair of Tacitus himself. Stoicism could at least provide a certain grandeur of stern fatalism of contempt for death as well as life; joined with the innate pessimism of the Epicurean, this strange cold gloom as of shadowy cypress groves, scattered here and there in the arid glare of the Senecan desert, was to attract and influence the more melancholy side of the Elizabethans—a Chapman, a Marston, a Webster.

> Nought after death, and death is nought,
> Of our swift race the final goal.
> Let Hope forget the dream it sought,
> And Fear forsake the weary soul.
> Where wilt thou lie when life is gone?
> With things unborn.   (*Troades* 397–9, 407–8.)

For indeed of Seneca the best is yet to be told. With his faults, his gross bad taste, his insincerity, his heartlessness and soullessness, his heart and soul are, to do him justice, not dead, but sleeping. And in the moments when they wake, for a few lines here, a chorus there, he writes poetry, the real thing.

As Quintilian says (x, 1, 125–31) "There is much that is praiseworthy, even admirable about him provided care is taken in selection—if only he had taken it himself." But the whole passage of Quintilian is too good not to be quoted. That fine critic is indeed thinking mainly of his prose and of that mainly from the oratorical point of view: but what he says is hardly less true of the tragedies.

He begins by contradicting the popular belief that he had a particular animus against Seneca. He admired the man, but he found his influence both enormous and dangerous—the youth of his day imitated only him and in him only his faults.

"There are many fine thoughts in Seneca," he proceeds, "and much useful morality, but his style is largely corrupt and most demoralising for the very reason that it is full of attractive literary vices. One wishes he had written under his own inspiration, but under someone else's criticism; for had he but despised certain tricks, and not hankered after certain perversions of style, had he not doted on whatever he wrote and not broken the force of everything he said by niggling niceties of thought, he would now be approved by the consensus of the educated instead of the *enthusiasm of the juvenile*; still, even so, he is worth reading for those of mature judgment who have been sufficiently trained in sterner stuff, if only because he provides, in any case, a useful exercise in criticism. For as I have said there is much that is praiseworthy, even admirable, about him, provided care is taken in selection,—if only he had taken it himself! For his gifts were worthy of higher aims; what he did aim at, he accomplished."

How fair, how grave, how gentlemanly it all is—the Roman at his best. One feels there is little left to say; but before we turn from Seneca the tragedian, last tottering pillar of the Classic stage, to the darkness of the barbarian and the Medieval Church and the morrow of the Renaissance, it is only just that his better self, Seneca the poet, should be heard.

Thus, though his style is generally smooth to tameness, so that its quiet manner in combination with the lurid matter of the plays has rather the incongruity of a demure little

Quaker maid swearing and blaspheming like a dragoon—yet he does at times obtain a certain splendour of sound.

> Lucis Suevi nobiles Hercyniis.
> Adulterum secuta per Symplegadas.

He knows the Miltonic glamour of proper names—"Whether in Aspromont or Montalban."

> Quolibet vento faciles Calydnae
> An carens numquam Gonoessa vento
> Quaeque formidat Borean Enispe.
>
> (*Troades* 839–41.)

> "To Calydnae's haven, in all winds easy,
> Or to where gale-swept Gonoessa towers,
> Or Enispe dreading the wild North-easter."

With all their monotony and clumsiness of metre his choruses sometimes reach an almost Horatian splendour of sonorousness.

> Audax ire vias irremeabiles
> Vidisti Siculae regna Proserpinae.
>
> Acheron invius
> Renavigari.

While sometimes, compound as he ever is of classic and romantic, ancient and modern, he seems to look forward to the lilting organ-roll of the Medieval Latin hymn.

> Nunc Phoebe mitte currus
> Nullo morante loro.
> Nox condat alma lucem,
> Mergat diem timendum
> Dux noctis Hesperugo.   (*Medea* 874–8.)

Then how graceful the memory he twines about the little port of Aulis! Tiphys the helmsman of the Argo was once her king; but he lies buried far in wastes of sandy Libya, and his native haven looks for his returning sails in vain.

> In a far, mean grave among strange ghosts he's lying,
>   But mindful of her king that comes no more,
> Aulis holds fast her mariners, vainly crying
>   To leave her windbound shore.   (*Medea* 621–4.)

It was at Aulis a few years later that the windbound Agamemnon was to sacrifice his own child to fill his sails for
Troy.

Then there is that oft-quoted anticipation of Columbus in
the *Medea*:

> An age shall come, as the world grows old,
> When Ocean shall fling his chains away,
> And a great new land to men unfold.
> Another world shall the deep display,
> And distant Thule cease to be
> The earth's utmost extremity.   (375–9.)

The man has imagination, could he but be natural; were
he content to feel, not to juggle with, his inspiration.

But, as was perhaps to be expected, it is in the context of
night and sleep and death and Hell that his naturally macabre
vision is most powerful and most itself.

In the description of Hades by Theseus in the *Hercules
Furens* (662–829) already mentioned, there are flashes of
imagination not unworthy the author of *Paradise Lost*. First
of all, come the Personifications who as in Virgil guard the
Nether Threshold, Sleep, and Famine and Fear, Death and
Grief and Age; and among them, a Spenserian figure,
"Belated Shame doth hide his guilty face." Then, as the lost
soul descends, the stagnant gloom gathers thicker:

> The house of death is worse than death itself.

There, girt by the streams of Styx and Acheron, sits Dis Himself,
dark brother of the Olympian Jupiter.

> Grim is his mien, with yet the noble stamp
> Of his high brother and his lofty race;
> Like Jove his face is, but a thundering Jove.   (723–5.)

In the ode that follows, the Chorus take up the description of the great army of the Hellward hastening dead—men old and in the flower of life, lads and lasses yet unwed, and last of all

> Small babes that have but learnt the name of mother.
>   For them alone, to spare their childish fears,
>   The gloom is lit with torchlight: every other
>   Treads that dark road in tears. (854–7.)

And then the Chorus breaks into that agonised question of the ages, "What is the thought in your hearts, O silent dead—when the last light is darkened and you feel that the earth has closed above your heads for ever?" And the dim reply comes ringing back in the Chorus of the *Troades*:

> The Nether World and the bitter reign
> Of tyrannous Dis and the fangs agleam
> Of the Hound of Hell—all rumours vain,
> All idle tales and an evil dream! (402–6.)

As for death even in the spurious and inferior *Hercules on Oeta* there is an anticipation of one of the finest things in Swinburne.

The Chorus sing of the end of the World.

> Death and Chaos that selfsame day
> All of the gods shall surely slay;
> Turning his doom on his own head
> Death shall himself at the last lie dead. (1114–17.)

So, twenty centuries after, *In a Forsaken Garden*:

> Here now in his triumph where all things falter,
> Stretched out on the spoils that his own hand spread
> Like a god self-slain on his own strange altar,
>   Death lies dead.

With other passages great enough to influence Shakespeare himself we shall be more relevantly concerned later. But in Seneca's honour one merits mention here.

It is an idea derived originally from Sophocles (*Oed. Tyrannus* 1227–8) and developed in the *Phaedra* (715–8) and the *Hercules Furens* (1323–8). In the second passage Hercules, restored to his senses after murdering his wife and children, cries in self-horror:

> What Tanais, what Nile or swirling flood
> Of Persian Tigris, what wild Rhine or Tagus,
> Rolling in spate the rich Iberian gold,
> Will wash this right hand clean? Though cold Maeotis
> Should deluge me with all her Arctic waves,
> Or all the Ocean flood across these hands,
> The stain of blood will stay.

Who does not know the echo in *Macbeth* (II, 2)? And Lady Macbeth's "all the perfumes of Arabia" carries on its bitter cry.

As usual Shakespeare's adaptation is "a planet greater than the sun that cast it." But if his gold makes Seneca seem but gilt—still here Seneca too is great. Let us take leave of him with those two great lines which close the *Medea* and which sum up the actual, though far from the professed, moral of Senecan, like not a little Elizabethan tragedy. It is the parting wail of the despairing Jason, above the bodies of his children, as Medea disappears in her dragon car:

> Go, sail the lofty spaces of high Heaven,
> A proof, where'er thou goest, that Gods are not.
>
> (*Medea* 1026–7.)

Provincial, pedant and prig, part Socrates, part Worldly Wiseman, part Grand Vizier, and yet always human, sometimes a poet, at the end a hero, none can indeed claim for Seneca that he was in any real sense first-rate; but though he could not himself enter the Holy Land, though he died within the marches of Philistia, his spirit was one day to be the guide and fiery beacon of the tragedy of all Western Europe.

CHAPTER IV

DARKNESS AND DAWN

"The flower of all writers" HEYWOOD of Seneca.
"Inferior in majesty to none of the Greeks, in culture and polish even greater than Euripides." SCALIGER.

WITH Seneca, Classic Tragedy gutters out; Rome's greatest historian, her greatest satirist were still to come; but the twilight has already darkened across her stage. Yet it was only drama, not histrionics, that died; all through the dusty decadence of the Western Empire the passion for pantomimes and ballet-dancers, however cursed by the church and scorned by the barbarians, ineradicably persists. Rome might be threatened with famine and all foreigners, even "professors of the liberal arts" expelled—three thousand ballet-girls were retained[1]; the Vandal might thunder at the gates of Carthage—with the groans of the dying mingled the delirious applause of her theatre. Equally vain were for long the fulminations of the Fathers of the Church. A husband might be allowed to divorce his wife for an unpermitted visit to the theatre; a devil who had entered a woman might refuse to be exorcised on the ground that she had been trespassing on his own demesne; that lewd-minded fiend Tertullian might gloat over the prospect of a tragedian screaming with real anguish, the comedian skipping with real nimbleness in the everlasting fires of the Last Day. It was a mockery of Christ, he cried, to add a cubit to a man's stature with a tragic buskin, it was defacing God's image to paint man's face, and it was contraverting Deuteronomy

[1] Amm. Marc. xiv, 6, 19.

xxii, 5 to wear women's clothes[1]—a fatuity destined to be monotonously echoed by sixteenth-century Puritanism; for indeed, the puritanically poor in spirit have never been notably blessed in invention. Yet in spite of all, Augustine still bears witness in the fifth century to a vitality in the theatre sufficient to empty the churches; and Sidonius after him. The Emperor, between the Church and the mob, compromised by laws at once stamping the professional actors and actresses in the mire of social degradation and making it as difficult as possible for them to leave that profession. Piety was propitiated, vulgarity continued to be pleased. The Roman world, said Salvianus, "moritur et ridet," laughs while it dies. Even in the sixth century Theodoric the Goth maintained a contemptuous toleration. Only in the seventh did the barbarians and the Christians finally triumph. The last of the actors took the road.

In the ferment of those dark ages the descendant of the despised Latin 'mimus' partly coalesced with the posterity of the honoured Teutonic 'scôp' or bard, whose position of dignified eminence recalls Homer's Demodocus in the court of King Alcinous. Hence sprang the 'joculator' or 'jongleur,' combined juggler and minstrel, like that Taillefer who rode before William the Norman up the hill of Senlac, throwing his sword in the air and catching it, while he sang of the Paladins of Charlemain. And as the Salvation Army presses the Devil's music-hall tunes into the service of its God, so St Francis' Minorites called themselves "joculatores Domini."

Then, in the eleventh century, in Provence arises beside the jongleur, the more literary 'trobair,' while the 'mimus' proper, the gesture-dancer, the 'bufo,' has remained his improper self all along[2].

---

[1] Tert. De Spect. xxx.
[2] Nor can we forget those jolly fellows, the 'scolares vagantes' (twelfth

The Church as persistently maintains a running fight with the forces of darkness. Cries Alcuin: "Set thy thoughts on chanting churchmen not on dancing bears." And a perpetual growl of ecclesiastic vituperation rumbles through the centuries that follow; not without reply from the minstrels, sometimes bitter, as when Aucassin cries to go, not to Heaven with the priests, but to Hell with his most sweet lady Nicolete; sometimes humorous, as in the tale of the minstrel in the Netherworld who lost so many souls at dice to St Peter that none of his trade have been allowed there since.

Now these merry folk are to provide one of the sources of the new drama; and their fifteenth century representatives are to become some of the first of its professional actors.

It is easy to see how recitation can become elementary drama, as the reciter speaks less and less in his own person, more and more in imaginary dialogue. From exchanges of quips like those between the King and the Minstrel in the fabliau of the "Jongleur d'Ely" (thirteenth century)—"How is that river called?" "No need to call it: it comes of itself," —from impersonations and mimicries of one's betters or the lower animals, the transition is easy if gradual to little dramatic sketches like "The Weeping Bitch," which dates from Edward I. A clerk is rejected by a damsel. He betakes himself to one Dame Siriz, who, after some mock piety, promises her aid. With a small bitch, encouraged to weep liberally by the application of mustard, she visits the damsel, and introduces it as her own daughter, unhappily bewitched to thirteen centuries) who took to the road and left their learning hanging in shreds on the wayside briars. As one of them lustily sings:

A Bouvines delez Dinant	"Hard by Dinant at Bouvines
Li perdi-je Ovide le grant.	Of Ovid there the last I've seen.
Mon Lucan et mon Juvenal	My Lucan and my Juvenal
Oubliai-je à Bonnival.	I left behind at Bonnival.
Eustace le grant et Virgile	The great Eustace and eke Virgil
Perdi au dez à Abévile.	I lost at dice at Abbéville."

by a clerk whom she likewise had once refused. The terrified damsel succumbs forthwith. The oldest English dramatic fragment (though not meant for acting) *The Harrowing of Hell*, written under Henry III, is itself but an "estrif" or debate between Christ and Satan.

From the thirteenth century we find Minstrels on the establishment of Noblemen; in the sixteenth they were to become My Lord's Players. For indeed with the advent of printing, the day of the true minstrel was done, though the 'mimus' is still going strong in the twentieth century.

Such is one source of the revival of drama, the only one preserving a continuity, however shadowy, all the way back to the Rome of the Caesars. For, in all, four original founts of modern drama may be traced; the Mimi, or Minstrels, the rustic Festivals, the liturgical drama of the Roman Church and the classical of the Renaissance. We are really concerned with the last; but the other three cannot be ignored.

Secondly, then, as ancient tragedy and comedy sprang from folk ritual, and comedy in particular from rustic buffooneries, so the medieval stage owes something to semi-christianized paganism like the May Game, the Robin Hood plays (that so English worthy being perhaps only a northern forest deity) and the Mummers' Plays like those called after St George— all connected originally with the changes of the year, the death of winter and summer's triumph. Above all, round Christmas and New Year clings the Feast of Fools with its offshoots, the Boy Bishop and the Lord of Misrule[1], who are still nearer kin of the winter kings of Fraser's *Golden Bough*.

The Feast of Fools flourished, especially in France, in the twelfth—thirteenth centuries, but was not extinct even in the seventeenth. An ass was led into the church, the celebrant

[1] Such as, at Cambridge, the "King of King's" and the "Emperor of Trinity," who are recorded in 1548 as making a state visit to Queens'.

brayed a mock Mass ("Ter hinhinnabit" say the Beauvais
directions), clerics danced dressed as women in the Choir,
black pudding was eaten and dice played on the altar, old
shoes were burnt in the censers. It was as in Pater's en-
chanting tale, Dionysus come back to the world of the "pale
Galilean"; and his players, too, were to reappear with him.
The serious ecclesiastic frowned at this annual reconquest
of the House of God by the old pagan orgies of the past.
But it corresponded to something innate in the medieval
mind, the grotesqueness which mingled with its fervour, the
wild laughter amid its tears, which manifests itself in perpetual incongruities of this sort, as in weird figures of a
Bere Regis or the gargoyles of a Notre Dame. So these
mummeries persisted long, even to 1645, among the
Franciscans of Antibes with their books held upside down
and their spectacles of orange-peel; and to this breaking
loose of pagan licence Drama owes something on its comic
side.

Far more important, however, is Drama's debt to the
hostile Church herself. In her services, as Ward points out,
the priest, the reading of the Gospel or Prophets, the anti-
phonal singing of the choir, already provide the dramatic epic
and lyric elements of Tragedy. Then, in the ninth and tenth
centuries, at the ceremonies of Easter, a touch of dialogue is
introduced: "Whom do ye seek?" "Jesus of Nazareth." "He
is not here. Go, say he is risen from the dead." Brethren
impersonate the angel at the sepulchre and the three Maries;
then the Apostles are brought in; then the risen Christ.
Similar elementary liturgic dramas gather round Christmas
and the shepherds, Innocents' Day and the massacre, the
Star in the East, Herod and the Kings; or the Prophets are
brought in to testify to the Godhead of Christ, and our old
friend the ass of the Feast of Fools now inserts himself
as Balaam's, made of wood and glorified with a human

voice by a boy concealed inside[1]. Medieval humour is incorrigible.

Once more, as Attic Tragedy most probably sprang from the honours paid to the consecrated dead at his tomb, but lost their local association and came out into the world, so the liturgic drama, first called into being at the sepulchre of Christ, by the fourteenth century has exchanged its Latin for the vernacular, become independent of the liturgic office, left the church for the market-place, and now clusters into the Guild Mystery-Cycles of the period: such as the York, Townley, Chester, and Coventry plays. To these a great impetus was given by the establishment of the festival of Corpus Christi in 1311 by Clement V.

This secularization was obvious and inevitable. As the religious drama grew in size laymen had to be called in as supplementary actors; like everything else, as it grew popular in one sense it had to become so in the other: Herod and the Devil became more and more comic, the Magdalen more and more romantic. Already in the Norman drama *Adam* no small degree of subtle humour has been attained. The serpent tempts Eve: "I saw Adam: he is an ass." "He *is* a little hard." "We shall melt him; at present he is harder than iron. But as for you—" and a long and luscious string of compliments follows.

We cannot enter into the fascinating details of Mystery plays with their slightly distorting atmosphere of a delightful nursery, which is sometimes in danger of making us forget the deadly earnestness which went hand in hand with this frivolity, and was really the condition of it. For only ages with a perfectly unbreakable faith can play football with it.

---

[1] In his honour at Rouen on Christmas Day they sang:
"Hez, sire asne, car chantez,
Belle bouche rechinez.
Vous aurez du foin assez
Et de l'avoine à manger."

It was not robustness that made Victorian religion screech
to feel a pea of blasphemy through ten mattresses of reveren-
tial cotton-wool. We cannot linger over fascinating ledgers
where "sowles savyd or dampnyd" are with a fine im-
partiality paid twenty pence for their pains, a "worme of
conscyence" threepence, God two and eightpence, Faustus
for cock-crowing threepence, while Hell is mended for twopence and there is fivepence for "setting the world on fire";
nor over the picture of their pageants—swarms of birds and
beasts let loose at the Creation, an Adam and Eve mother-
naked before an astonished audience; or over the humour of
Noah wishing he had made his wife a ship "for herself
alone[1]"; or the pathos of little Isaac before his sacrifice:

> Now farwyll, my owne fader so fyne,
> And grete wyll my moder in erde.
> But I prey you, fader, to hide my eyne
> That I se not the stroke of your scharpe swerde,
> That my fleysse schall defyle.

But in its absolute unclassicism the Mystery is important
for the study of the Elizabethans. Only because the popular
dramatic instinct was so strongly developed in England did
the classical pedants, with Seneca for their fetish and a
misunderstood Aristotle for their war-cry, fail to shackle the
English stage with their ridiculous conventions and unities.
What were the unities to a race fresh from seeing four
thousand years in the compass of a spring day, the forty
days of the Flood elapsing while Noah shut and opened a
window, Rome, Jerusalem and Marseilles set out on scaffolds
almost touching one another?—or pedantic accuracy to those
who had watched Sir Lancelot massacring the Innocents,
heard Herod swearing by Mahound and the shepherds at
the Nativity by the death of Christ? And lastly, we owe the

[1] "Fighting ad lib." is one of the Townley stage directions during their
conjugal dialogue.

porter in *Macbeth*, the wild laughter of *Hamlet*, that whole
magnificent deepening of tragedy by the right contrast of
comic interlude, to the indifference of the sixteenth-century
populace to the *a priori* laments of Sidney and the cultured
over their "thrusting in of clowns by the head and shoulders
with neither decencie nor discretion"; this "mungrell Tragy-
comedie," this mingling of "Hornpypes and Funeralls[1]." It
is just this comic relief that is the soul of the Mystery; and
the Mystery consecrated it into a tradition strong enough to
cry in Chaucer's words:

> Straw for thy Senec and thy proverbis.

The comic boy, the "stynkynge eurdeyn" of the Hegge
Noah and Lamech, the spouse of Noah, the ass Burnell
who swears 'Perdy' in the Chester *Balaak and Balaam*, the
comic soldiers of the York *Resurrection Play*, the comic ostler
of the Digby *Conversion of St Paul*, the comic servant in the
Play of the Sacrament who thus proclaims his master the
doctor's merits:

> He had a lady late in cure;
> I wot by this she is full sure.
> There shall never Christian creature
> 　　Here hyr tell no tale,

and, "he will never leave you till ye be in your grave,"—all
this goodly army was too strong for the academic critic with
his "Aristorchus' eye," for the classical Pharisee with his
things "common and unclean." And yet these classicists did
not know their own case; Seneca never laughs, but greater
examples than Seneca were there; they forgot the old nurse
of the *Choephoroe*; forgot, too, the messenger of the *Antigone*
and the *Bacchae*, the Heracles of the *Alcestis*. However, it
was vain for them to rebuke their countrymen as Virgil
Dante:

> Che voler ciò udire è bassa voglia,

---

[1] Similarly, Milton in the preface to *Samson Agonistes*.

for the Englishman of the Middle Ages, whose gaiety strangers used to contrast unfavourably with the gravity of the French, had not yet learned to take his pleasures sadly.

We have said that comic relief was the soul of the Mysteries; that is too strong; it was indeed their great and growing attraction; but this merriment is itself only part of a greater thing, without which Elizabethan drama would have been as sickly a weed as contemporary French tragedy. It is part of that intensity of emotion about life which alone can produce the greatest work. As Anatole France says of Napoleon: "Il pensait ce que pensait tout grenadier de son armée, mais il le pensait avec une force inouïe." It may manifest itself in the jollity of a Chaucer or a Dickens, "fresh as is the month of May"; or in the titanic pessimism of the author of *Lear*. At the bottom it is the same—an emotional vitality, which whether it curses God or blesses him, lives and wills to live—

Unto the end, whatever be the end.

Shakespeare might in darker moments speak of "desiring this man's art or that man's scope"; Ben Jonson might echo that Shakespeare wanted art; but what makes Seneca and his strict English imitators as motes and pismires beside the great Elizabethans of the popular stage, is that in these survives still, however gilded and coloured by the Renaissance, the vehement emotional significance, the terror, the longing and the laughter which illumine the crudities of the fourteenth-fifteenth century Mystery Plays. Art, like the giant Antaeus, must ever and again renew its vitality by contact with the mother earth.

At the risk of being long and irrelevant I must sketch what indeed has so often been sketched before, the Townley *Secunda Pastorum*, as an example worth pages of criticism, of the native stock on which the classical drama was to be grafted so happily.

It is the night of the Nativity. One by one the three shepherds appear, soliloquizing; the first on the iniquity of rich men to poor; the second on the imprudence of marriages in general and his own in particular:

> I have oone to my fere, (wife)
> As sharp as a thystyll, as rugh as a brere;

the third on the weather, which appears as English as himself:

> Was never syn Noe floode sich floodys seyn.

Then arrives one Mak, of ill-repute as a sheep-stealer, who is put to bed in the middle of them as a precaution against his sleep-walking after mutton; which does not prevent him appearing shortly after at his wife's door with a sheep on his back. For concealment the creature is wrapped up in the cradle, as if it were a new-born child: then Mak goes back and lies down in his place. In the morning there is a hue-and-cry for the missing sheep; they search the house, but the sick mother makes such an outcry and swears so forcibly:

> I pray God so mylde,
> If ever I you begylde,
> That I ete this chylde
> That lygys in this credyll;

that the shepherds hastily depart. Then one is touched with a kindly thought and turns back:

Tertius Pastor. Mak, with your lefe, let me gyf your barne
              Bot sexpence.
Mak.   Nay, do way, he slepys.
Pastor. Me thynke he pepys.
Mak.   When he wakyns he wepys,
        I pray you go hence.
Pastor. Gyf me lefe hym to kys, and lyft up the clowtt.
        What the devill is this? he has a long snowte!

They make laughing remarks on the persistence of heredity; then realise it is their sheep:

> Sagh I never in a credyll
> A hornyd lad or now.

They proceed to toss the red-handed Mak in a sheet—when suddenly is heard the "Gloria in excelsis" of the angelic host. They turn and go and bring their humble offerings—"a bob of cherrys," "a byrd" and a ball to the new-born, the "lytyll day-starre," in the manger of Bethlehem.

So it ends—crude, incongruous, ill-constructed, and yet what is more than all, livingly human. Drury Lane in the twentieth century would doubtless have done it with real Bedouin and live camels. But it was this unvarnished humanity of the Middle Ages that was to add life to academic humanism, to the resurrected bones of the Classical tradition. The gift of Antiquity, our debt to Seneca in particular is not to be written off; thence were to come the five-act play, the essential unity of action as well as the idle unities of place and time, new plots, new legends, new types of character[1], a new type of dialogue, a new metre of infinite possibilities. But all these must have been but "a breath of grave and a skinful of dead men's blood" without the living soul, the stark, undirected energy of Medieval England, still unsicklied with academic thought, still unashamed of intense and simple emotions, still rooted in the "good, gross earth" of a young and vital virility.

Thus from the tenth to the thirteenth centuries the religious drama develops in the bosom of the Church; in the fourteenth it definitely passes from Church to Market-place,

[1] Not all new, however. The Elizabethan Tyrant is not so much nearer to the typical Senecan than to the equally orgulous Augustus or Tiberius, proud of being able to speak Latin, or King of Marcylle with his "lawdabyll presens," or Herod shouting "Owt! Owt!! Owt!!!" as he "rages in the pagond and in the strete." And the sententious moralizing, and even a sort of stichomuthia are not unknown there.

from the clergy to the laity of the municipal guilds; and in
the fifteenth there is a further gradual transition from the
resident amateurs of the Guilds with their Mysteries to the
strolling professionals of Morality and Interlude, from
Market-place to Banquet-hall. Just so in the sixth century
B.C. Thespis had freed tragedy from the local ties of his
native deme and taken the first step in the evolution of drama
from ritual to art.

The rise of the Morality may be linked with the growing
love of allegory, already evident in the *Romaunt of the Rose*
and *Piers Plowman*. Allegorical figures like Dolor and
Myserye in the Norwich *Creacion Play*, had prepared the
way for this new form, consisting, in Jusserand's words "of
the debates and *disputoisons* of former days turned into
drama. The Virtues recommended virtue, Nature explained
the mysteries of nature, and Satan advised the audience not
to follow his advice." As might be expected, these edifying
productions are for the most part exceedingly tedious, save
for a few pleasant lyrics like:

> Now I wyll follow Folye
> For Folye is my man,

in *Mundus et Infans*, and the laudable

> O the body of me,
> What caytyves be those
> That wyll not once flee
> From Tediousnes' nose,

of *Wyt and Science*; except also for the Vices and Devils,
the new incarnation of the Comic Spirit. So the audience
too appears to have felt; in *Mankind* when the devil Tytivillus
begins to ramp and roar behind the scenes, then is the time
to send round the hat.

> Gyf us rede reallys yf ye wyll se hys abbomynabull presens.

But the Morality could not exist on pure edification. It
became a medium of religious polemic like Bale's *King John*,

precursor of the Elizabethan History Play, a most curious farrago of abstractions and historical persons, or an instrument of political criticism as in Lindsay's *Three Estates*, or lastly of pure amusement, as in the *Interludes* of Heywood (1497-1577).

Here the first breath of Renaissance Classicism is felt. Plautus godfathers the transition between these Interludes and the first regular comedies *Ralph Roister Doister* and *Gammer Gurton's Needle*, that most true and happy blend of English life and classic form.

Similar is the development of regular Tragedy. With the growing knowledge of classical history and legend we find on the popular stage strange amorphous hybrids like *Horestes* (1565), *Appius and Virginia* (1575) and *King Cambises*, destined by-word for bombast (1569). There, amid the worthies of Herodotus, beside the ferocious tyrant who has Sisamnes flayed alive on the stage, skips and jeers the homely English Vice of the Morality just as in *Damon and Pithias* (1571), Grim, the collier of Croydon, lurches and "singeth Basse" about the court of Dionysius at Syracuse. The gods must have their laugh; but this type of play was to die of it. As Brooke has said, English Tragedy was to arise not from the classicising of Native, but from the naturalisation of Classic, Drama.

We have dealt with the growth of the Native Element in Elizabethan Tragedy from the ninth century liturgic drama, through Mystery, Morality, and Interlude, with the awakening of a popular dramatic spirit by the Minstrels descended from the Mimes of Rome, and with Folk Rituals derived from immemorial paganism. It remains to resume our main thread—the influence of the Classics.

After the unknown poet Magnus, pompously said by Sidonius in the fifth century to have "outdone insolent Greece and haughty Rome," the drama as we have seen

vanishes into darkness. The next name is the tenth century
nun Hrotsvitha of Gandersheim, who wrote Terentian plays
on edifying religious subjects in Latin rhymes of incredible
insipidity. However their influence appears to have been
negligible. The atmosphere of an age when Leo, the Papal
Legate could speak of "Plato, Virgil, Terence and the other
beasts of philosophers" and Odo of Cluny likened Virgil to
"a beautiful vase, full of noxious serpents," was too in-
clement.

Terence himself did indeed survive through the Darkest
Ages with a curious and unique vitality: but the whole idea
of Tragedy and Comedy underwent the most ludicrous
distortions. The plays of Terence were supposed to have
been recited from a pulpit by one Calliopius[1] while actors
did dumb show beneath; and similarly Seneca's[2]. Further,
that Tragedy or Comedy had anything particular to do with
acting, was quite forgotten. Before 450 Dracontius could call
his epic *Orestes* a tragedy. Isidore (died 636) calls Horace,
Persius, and Juvenal 'tragedians.' The idea took root that any
dignified narrative with an unhappy ending was a Tragedy;
and conversely anything ending happily was comedy. Dante's
own *Divina Commedia*, beginning in Hell and ending in
Paradise, is the classic instance. Johannes Anglicus (c. 1260)
names Ovid as the one Latin tragedian and supplies a second
tragic specimen of his own invention which he much commends[3]. There are besieged sixty soldiers and two washer-
women, that is, one to thirty soldiers. A soldier of one
section, however, is caught by his washerwoman with her
rival; she slays them both and lets in the enemy.

Dante himself is not a great deal wiser; tragedy, he says,
means "goat-song," that is "noisome as a goat." His

[1] A third or fourth century commentator on Terence, antedated five
or six hundred years.
[2] So Treveth (1260–1330).
[3] J. W. Cunliffe, *Early English Classical Tragedy*, pp. ix–xiv.

commentator Francesco da Buti went one better—"As a goat is bearded and august before and bare behind, so a tragedy begins with prosperity and ends in nakedness[1]."

That is indeed the other side of the Middle Ages, spiritual and emotional richness, material and intellectual penury. Humanity in general has been likened to the little children Martin Doul speaks of in Synge's *Well of the Saints*—who

> do be listening to the stories of an old woman and do be dreaming often in the dark night that it's in grand houses of gold they are, with speckled horses to ride, and do be waking again in a short while and they destroyed with the cold and the thatch dripping, maybe, and the starved ass braying in the yard.

Of no period is this so true as of the Dark Ages—Le gente dolorose che hanno perduto il ben dell' intelletto.

But the night was growing grey. On Dec. 3, 1315, Albertino Mussato was crowned with laurel before the University and citizens of Padua for his Senecan Latin play, *Ecerinis*, a work recited not acted, which dealt with the career of the fiendish Ezzelino III, lord of Padua. It is the fountain head of Modern Classical Drama.

Yet the development was slow. Not till the beginning of the sixteenth century does Tragedy really come to life in Italy, not till the middle of it in France and England. Yet it was in England, the most distant and latest field, that the seed of Senecan tragedy came soonest to harvest: and only later were Racine in France, Alfieri in Italy to produce a type of tragedy even nearer the Senecan original. The reason is not far to seek. In Italy and France dramatic art was, for the present, killed with culture. In neither was there a theatre-going populace numerous and obstinate enough to like what it liked, not what it was told to like, and to insist on having that. Their atmosphere was darkened instead with

---

[1] Chambers, *Medieval Stage*, 2, 209.

legions of critics, Cinthios and Scaligers. As Symmes[1] says:

Les théoriciens dramatiques en France et en Italie au sixième siècle sont nombreux et souvent ingénieux. En Angleterre ils sont peu nombreux, leurs écrits ne sont pas très profonds et relativement, Sidney et Jonson exceptés, ils sont presque insignifiants.

We may thank Heaven for it! Dramatic theoreticians are about as competent to teach a dramatist how to create living plays, as old gentlemen who have spent devoted years chopping up dead frogs, to instruct live ones how to create tadpoles. England had no Richelieus to demonstrate the beneficent effect on art of politicians not content to mismanage their own business, no drivelling pedants of the type that fussed over the audacity of Racine in ending a play with "Hélas!" his vulgarity in concealing Nero behind a curtain, his lowness in speaking of "des *chiens* dévorants." Hence, while these Solomons of France and Italy were hunting up precedents, the poets of England were creating them. It was well for Lope de Vega and Webster, despite their complaints, that they had to "lock up the precepts with six keys," since "the breath of the uncapable multitude" could poison the correctest raptures.

In consequence the sixteenth century dramatists of France and Italy, fed on the carefully sterilised milk of this Senecan tradition, produced dull trash of a kind that was tolerated nowhere in England outside the Inns of Court and the Universities of Oxford and Cambridge.

Somehow a goose is none the less a goose,
Though moon and stars be mixed to yield it stuffing.

The *Ecerinis*, then, of 1315 though its action covers a period of forty-six years, is otherwise typically Senecan with its

[1] Quoted by J. W. Cunliffe, *Early English Classical Tragedy*, pp lxvi–lxvii.

ferocious tyrant, its chorus, its Devil-raising, and its no less than five messengers.

In 1387 follows the *Achilleis* of Antonio de' Loschi of Verona.

In 1429 Corraro of Mantua wrote a *Progne*—Ovid's story with the cannibalism of Seneca's *Thyestes*.

In 1485 Pomponius Laetus revived the acting of Classical Tragedies and Comedies at Rome. In the same year Seneca's Tragedies were first printed in Paris.

In 1499 was acted at Ferrara the *Filostrato e Panfila* of Cammelli, the first tragedy in Italian, Senecan, but showing Medieval influence both in the Romance of its Boccaccian story—the same on which the English *Gismond of Salerne* is based—and in its resemblance to the methods of the religious drama.

It is becomingly introduced by the Ghost of Seneca himself, and has his five Acts with choruses between, two confidants, a dream and a vision.

In 1515 was written Trissino's *Sofonisba*, modelled on the Greeks, rather than Seneca, whose five act structure it ignores. It has however the inevitable dream, the inevitable confidante, and also five messengers. Such was the price of the unities; as Ogier, the one sane French critic, wrote (1628) "Much fitter is it for a renowned inn, than for an excellent tragedy, to be frequented by abundance of messengers."

It was acted in France in 1556, in Italy in 1562 with scenery by Palladio and eighty actors—the sort of fate it deserved. In 1541 was acted, also at Ferrara, whose dukes had money and extravagance enough to go on gilding this ever staler gingerbread, the *Orbecche* of Giraldi Cinthio. Cinthio was also a critic, less hide-bound than most; he pleads timidly to be allowed to innovate just a little; of his taste, typical of his class and time, it is sufficient to say that it noisily preferred Seneca to all the Greeks.

His tragedy is accordingly introduced by Nemesis and the Furies, then follows the ghost of Selina; Chorus, Nuntius, and Counsellor are as usual; at the end the stage becomes the traditional abattoir.

Lastly Dolce (1508–68) translated amongst other classics Seneca and the *Phoenissae* of Euripides, his version of which was in turn rendered into English by Gascoigne and performed at Gray's Inn in 1566. We can turn to France.

About 1540–45 the exiled Scot Buchanan had produced at Bordeaux not only Latin translations of Euripides, but two original Latin Biblical tragedies, *Jepthes* and *Baptistes*. Among the amateur actors of his plays was a certain young rogue, the Sieur Michel de Montaigne. In 1552–3 appeared Jodelle's *Cléopatre*—ghost, vision, confidant, messenger, and all. Senecan influence increased. In Garnier, the next name of importance (eight tragedies 1563–90), it is paramount. Garnier's effect on the English academic coterie of the Countess of Pembroke, Kyd, Brandon, Daniel, in producing a second wave of English Senecanism must be dealt with later.

The first influence of Seneca in England was naturally felt in the schools and universities, and the first imitations of him, as in Italy and France, were composed in Latin. In 1532 the boys of St Paul's acted before Cardinal Wolsey a Latin tragedy on Dido by their headmaster, one of the becoming name of Rightwise. About ten years later, and simultaneously with Buchanan's Latin Bible plays in France, appeared the *Absalom* of Watson, which he suppressed, as Ascham says, on account of minor metrical lapses, and the *Christus Redivivus* of Grimald, acted at Oxford in 1540, which however is full of comic soldiers and rather a combination of Terence and Medievalism than a Senecan play. In the years 1550–63 the Cambridge records become very Senecan:

his *Troades* and *Medea* are twice acted, his *Oedipus*[1] once, at
Trinity. During the same period, in 1561, at the Christmas
Revels of the Inner Temple was performed at Westminster
the first English play in the Senecan form, the first regular
English tragedy, the first English drama in blank verse[2]—
Gorboduc. Its authors Norton and Sackville were graduates
of Oxford: doubtless there was a tense and aromatic atmosphere of extreme culture and supreme refinement about
this most memorable of Christmas plays. Which does not
prevent it being extremely dull reading, much as Sidney
admired it and Pope praised its chaste correctness and gravity,
so misunderstood or neglected, alas, by later tragic poets like
Shakespeare. Gorboduc divides Britain between his two
sons, who are rivals like Eteocles and Polynices; the elder is
murdered by the younger; their mother murders him in turn;
the people rise and murder her and Gorboduc; a civil war
follows. The play does not observe the unities and the last
act is so concerned with edifying Queen Elizabeth into
marriage that it has the most tenuous connexion with the
plot. The play is equipped with a very Senecan cast of
corresponding characters—the King has his counsellor, each
of the rival sons has his, as well as a wicked parasite who
nullifies the counsellor's sententious and interminable
wisdom. There are three messengers' speeches and a Chorus
of "foure auncient and sage men of Brittaine" laments
between the Acts. The authors murder their characters with
a restrained economy of horrors: on the other hand none of
them except Marcella, the secret of whose heart Lamb
surprised in his charming way, was ever really alive. The play
belongs rather to antiquarianism than literature.

For the next half century the academies of the Universities

---

[1] Unless they are original neo-Senecan plays on those subjects.

[2] English blank verse was first used by Surrey to represent the Virgilian hexameter, then here for the Senecan iambic.

and Inns of Court go on producing their ephemeral Latin and English tragedies, while the popular playwrights having stolen their classic thunders conquer for themselves an abiding place in English Literature.

Thus the Queen was entertained with a *Dido* at Cambridge in 1564, a *Progne* at Oxford two years later. The latter opened with the ghost of the Thracian Diomede foaming at the mouth and baited by Furies with torches to prologise the doom of his own house, exactly like the ghost of Tantalus in Seneca's *Thyestes*. With Tudor unsqueamishness the audience then proceeded to watch Tereus dining off his son's flesh on the stage. This play is fortunately not extant.

In 1579 was produced at Cambridge a Senecan tragedy on Richard III, by Legge, the Master of Caius, which influenced *The True Tragedie of Richard III*, which in its turn affected Shakespeare's play, one of his most Senecan. It has therefore some adventitious interest though its importance has been unduly puffed. It is written in three Actiones, has hosts of characters, and disregards the unities entirely; but it is full of Senecan tags, and the complaint of the Queen-mother as she gives up the little Duke of York is based closely on Andromache's lament over Astyanax in the *Troades*. But Legge's was a poverty-stricken mind; his Latin versification might crimson the cheek of a preparatory schoolboy; and but for the sad fact that by the time they have read sufficiently to write on English Literature, scholars have only too often lost the gift, unhappily for their readers, of knowing what is boring and what is not, this fatuous production of a shallow pedant would have been treated with as little respect as it deserves[1].

---

[1] It may be added that John Palmer of St John's who took the part of Richard "had his head so possest with a prince-like humour" that he behaved like a potentate ever after, and died in prison as the result of his regal prodigalities.

Of a far finer stamp are the plays of Gager of Christchurch, *Meleager* (1581), *Dido* (1583), and *Ulysses Redux* (1591). The first is based on Ovid and in worth may stand to Swinburne's *Atalanta*, as Seneca's *Agamemnon* to Aeschylus', it is not without vigour and merit: *Dido* is a not unhappy iambicising of the *Aeneid*, and the *Ulysses* a far more successful dramatisation of the end of the *Odyssey*.

It is indeed Seneca's Ulysses, not Homer's, who gloats:

> Praegestit animus latera transfixos humi
> Videre stratos: aspicere mensas libet
> Tabo fluentes, aspicere pateras libet
> Cerebro madentes. Spem tibi hanc intus fove.
> Hostem iuvat ridere: quanto plus iuvat
> Mactare: non est suavius spectaculum
> Hoste interempto.

> "My soul doth lust to see them strew the ground,
> Spears thro' their hearts: to see their tables run
> With human blood, to see their goblets wet
> With human brains. Cherish this dream, my soul.
> 'Tis sweet to mock a foe, but how much sweeter
> To slaughter him. There is no sight more joyous
> Than a slain enemy."

But Gager was not shackled to Seneca: he was not afraid to introduce a comic Irus or a Ulysses in rags. And even his pale classicism is tinged with romance: the handmaiden Melantho, mistress of Eurymachus, one of the chief of Penelope's suitors, as she is led out to be hanged, bewails her lot, with an echo of the dying Hadrian.

> Animula quae mox dulcis invises loca
> Pallidula, tremula, nudula? Haud posthac dabis
> Ut ante ludos, vagula, petulans, blandula,
> Non veste molli gesties, non tu dapes
> Gustabis ore, dulce non vinum bibes;
> Furtiva nullus oscula Eurymachus dabit.

"Ah little soul, whither departest thou,
Pallid one, timid one, naked one? No more
Shalt play as of old, wandering one, saucy one,
Coaxing one, nevermore go proudly clad,
Nor taste sweet wine nor pleasant food again;
And no Eurymachus thy kisses steal."

And when the last line, amongst other things was seized on by Rainolds of Corpus Christi, a fiery Puritan, as one of those flagrancies which made acting for undergraduates as heinous as "to play at Mum-chance or Maw with idle boon companions or at trunkes in guile-houses or to dance about Maypoles or to rifle in ale-houses or to carouse in taverns or to steale deer or to rob orchards," Gager took up the challenge and showed he could write for the humanities as well as in them.

In the next year, 1592, was acted at Trinity, Cambridge, Alabaster's *Roxana*, an adaptation of Groto's *La Dalida*; before we leave the University stage we may sketch its plot for the sake of the light it throws on the taste and style of the time. Written by a far better Latinist and cleverer man than Legge, it is yet a "reductio ad absurdum" of the pure Senecan play. The ghost of Molo, king of Bactria, who has been murdered by his nephew Oromasdes, and the Spirit of Suspicion speak the prologue. Bessus, Oromasdes' councillor, seduces Atossa, his wife, by revealing that Oromasdes has for ten years been the lover of his murdered predecessor's daughter Roxana. The jealous Atossa entraps and murders her rival Roxana and her two children; then, after she has banqueted her husband on their flesh, she reveals the truth; he counters by producing her lover Bessus' head. Each has already poisoned the other and they die raving. At the horror of it all, as we have said, a gentlewoman in the audience "fell distracted and never recovered."

Alabaster has all the morbidity and some of the cleverness

of Seneca himself. The cannibal husband and father mourns
in Gilbertian vein that having consumed a wife and two
children he has now a fourfold body and a fourfold grief and
that he goes to hell a fourfold ghost. A messenger narrates
how Atossa has murdered her victims and now prepares their
flesh for Oromasdes' table: it ends

> *Nuntius*, dabit sepulchrum. *Chorus*, vile? *Nuntius*, regium
> nimis.
> "*Mess.* A tomb she'll give. *Chorus*, a mean one? *Mess.* Nay,
> *too* royal." (Orosmasdes is to eat them.)

An interesting innovation is the Oxford English play
Caesar's Revenge (about 1594), the first sign of the reaction
of the popular stage on the Academic. For it imitates in
reason and out Kyd's *Spanish Tragedy*. But we cannot dwell
longer on what after all soon became a dramatic backwater.
The universities did their part for tragedy in introducing into
England that Senecan influence which spread by way of the
Inns of Court to the popular theatres, and in educating many
of the popular playwrights, like Marlowe, Greene, Nash and
Peele. And, as Boas also points out, the noble patrons of
actor companies must have been affected by the theatricals
of their undergraduate days. Not indeed that the universities
had any such good intentions; the popular stage from the
beginning was beneath the contempt of learned dons. Oxford,
for instance, from 1587–93 paid blackmail to the strolling
companies of players to keep them away from Oxford; Gager
in the heat of controversy with the anti-theatrical Rainolds
holds out the olive-branch of a common loathing of 'his-
triones,' professional actors; and Part I of the *Return from
Parnassus* gibes bitterly at the greatest Elizabethans from
Shakespeare and Ben Jonson downwards.

Meanwhile Seneca himself was seen in English verse:
between 1559–67 eight plays rendered by Jasper Heywood
and others had appeared; a collected edition of all ten was

published in 1581. At the same time the Inns of Court had been continuing their English Classical Plays. To *Gorboduc* the landmark of 1561, succeeded in 1566 *Jocasta*, Gascoigne's version of Dolce's version of Euripides' *Phoenissae*, in 1567–8 *Gismond of Salerne*, in 1588 Hughes' *Misfortunes of Arthur*, the most slavishly Senecan of all English plays.

Jocasta has a chorus of four gentlewomen, corresponding to the four ancients of *Gorboduc*, and similar dumb shows or charades before each Act, a non-classical feature of early English tragedies derived probably from the intermedii of Italian Renaissance tragedy, that is, little dances or shows between Acts; but they spring partly too, perhaps, from the native English love of pageantry. The shows in *Jocasta* are sufficiently various—Sesostris of Egypt, a flaming grave, Curtius the Roman, the Horatii and Curiatii and unstable Fortune. It is a painstaking but not exciting work.

Gismond is more interesting as the first combination of the Romantic Italian Renaissance love story with the classic form of Seneca. Tancred so dotes on his widowed daughter Gismond that he will not let her marry again. Having caught her with her lover, he puts him to death and sends his heart to Gismond in a goblet. She takes poison and Tancred then kills himself. Only Boccaccio's fine tale is sadly spoiled by the passion for edification which struggles with, though it does not entirely overcome, natural sympathy for the ill-fated lovers. There are more dumb-shows, more chorus, more Senecan epigrams from the commonplace book; Cupid descends from Heaven, Megaera rises from Hell. It is significant of the progress of taste that the second edition (1591) replaces rhyme with blank verse, and the final speech of Tancred, where he announces his intended suicide, by actual self-blinding and self-murder on the stage. Of such rough-hewn stuff was a later hand to shape plays like *Romeo and Juliet*.

The *Misfortunes of Arthur* was played in 1588. By then it is already a survival. A list of its Senecan passages with their Latin parallels takes up no less than 25 large pages in Cunliffe's laborious work. We are approximating to the type of writer who could amuse himself with writing the life of Christ in Virgil's hexameters. Arthur's son by his own sister, Mordred, during Arthur's wars in France, seduces his queen Guenevere. On Arthur's return she flies to a nunnery and after much talk and debate a great battle is fought in Cornwall, in which 120,000 fall and 20 on each side survive: then Arthur slays Mordred and receives his own death-wound.

The play opens and ends with the Senecan ghost of Gorlois, gloating over the usual revenge; it abounds in Senecan stichomuthia; its dumb-shows have become charades, foreshadowing the acts to follow, of an incredible complexity; its attempts at pathos or terror fall into the queerest bathos or bombast. The chorus blesses humble happiness.

How safe and sound the careless Snudge doth snore.

The Nuntius describes the last great battle in the West.

The weapons hide the Heavens: a night composed
Of warrelike Engines overshades the field.
From every side these fatale signes are sent
And boystrous bangs with thumping thwacks fall thicke.

In short it is the *reductio ad absurdum* of its predecessors. There is indeed a promise of greater things in Arthur's last words:

This only now I crave, (O Fortune erst
My faithfull friend), let it be soone forgot
Nor long in minde nor mouth where Arthur fell.
Yea, though I Conqueror die and full of Fame,
Yet let my death and parture rest obscure.
No grave I neede (O Fates) nor buriale rights,

Nor stately hearse nor tomb with haughty toppe.
But let my carkasse lurke; yea let my death
Be ay unknown, so that in every coast
I still be fear'd and lookt for every houre.

But it and its class had already ceased to signify.

The hour had struck though they heard not the bell.

In 1586 the theatre had acclaimed to the echo Kyd's *Spanish Tragedy*: in 1587 the boards quaked under the tread of *Tamburlaine*. Tragedy stood crowned on the English stage.

We have now reached the crucial point in the long line of descent from Seneca to Shakespeare—the union of the classical with the popular stage, of which the first offspring was to be that typical and proverbially popular melodrama, Kyd's *Spanish Tragedy*. We have traced the Senecan revival in Italy, France, and learned England, by writers as academic and therefore as barren as himself; now for the first time the seed falls on the solid earth of the English popular stage. The classicised interlude, like *Horestes* and *Cambises* was destined to wither; its classicism was too superficial; it had not learned the classical five act structure, the importance of Form; its comedy, the buffoonery of its Vice, was too uproariously clownish for Tragedy to make her voice properly heard. That is, the attempt to raise the Medieval horse-play to the height of the classical Olympus had failed; but the bringing down of the classical tragedy from that thin and pallid atmosphere to firm English ground was on the contrary to result in the most vital impulse in the history of English literature. So happy was the union of classical Artistry and refinement with Romantic life and vigour, of the classic sense of form and simplicity with the Romantic love of colour and luxuriance, of the classic care for words and style[1] with the Romantic insistence on action, on 'drama' as doing, not

[1] Cf. Ben Jonson's "Words above action; matter above words."

talking, lastly of Ancient humanism and tragic depth with Medieval religious intensity and comic relief. English Legend and History or Italian romance provided the human actors; the classic drama its background of Fate and Nemesis. The classic tradition established the conventions of Blank Verse, of five Acts, of Moralising and Introspection, Rhetoric and Stichomuthia, Ghosts and the Supernatural. The Medieval spirit, on the other hand, jettisoned the Unities and the restriction of the number of characters (there are forty in *Henry V*); it added the vital interest of Romantic love. This combination and compromise, this preference of common-sense to logic, are typically English; it was not the accident of the mediocrity of Alexandre Hardy that prevented any French counterpart of the Romantic drama of sixteenth century England. Classicism is too inherent in the French character: despite a Victor Hugo the spirit which made Voltaire dismiss Shakespeare as a "God-intoxicated barbarian," can still in the year 1920 move an Associate of the Académie Française to condemn Thomas Hardy to second-rateness on the ground of deficiency in art[1]. But the English comment on the classic drama is Pepys' entry on Jonson's *Catiline*: "A play of much good sense and words to read, but the least diverting that ever I saw any. And therefore home with no pleasure at all, except in sitting next to Betty Hall."

Elizabethan drama is then a fusion typical of England; but of Renaissance England. We have spoken hitherto of the restraining influence of the Classic; but it must not be forgotten that it had itself liberated the energies it restrained. If the classical influence of the Renaissance had set a yoke upon the artist to his good, it had also liberated the thinker; if, in that age English playwrights wrote like angels and worked like devils, and English popular audiences appreciated

[1] *Athenaeum*, Nov. 25, 1920.

their greatness in a way apparently impossible alike to their ancestors and to posterity, it was because the rediscovery of the Ancient World had redressed the balance of the Medieval, adding to its dark chaos of emotional and spiritual fervour the piercing light of the emancipated intellect. One cannot understand Elizabethan drama, without grasping the spirit of the Renaissance. The world had grown to undreamed vastness by the finding of a new continent, beyond the Atlantic; had dwindled to insignificance as a tiny ball whirling in the immensities of space. The old wine of Dionysus burst the restraints of Christian asceticism: Apollo with his self-knowledge and his self-control quelled the monster-haunted flamboyance of the Goth. Yet though the Renaissance artist learnt thus to fit his art within a straiter framework, the self-control was of all the lessons of antiquity the least well learned by the Renaissance man. The reaction from the iron repressions of Medievalism was too violent; humanism, freedom, directness, the frantic love of beauty, omnivorous versatility, these were the acceptable gospel of the New Paganism. God was dethroned; Man lifted newly-awakened, fearless eyes towards a Heaven that lowered no more; and the first-born of this new Humanism was a new and unashamed Individualism. Cultured and many-sided, men realised and treasured personality. The laws of God and man bent before the onrush of a new and infinite will to live, to drain life to the lees. Luther's *Pecca fortiter* is the motto of the age; such is the 'virtù' of Machiavelli; the Renaissance man is not of those who lack the faith to dis-believe, the character to commit crime, the vitality to be more than virtuous. It is an age of great rather than of good men. Lorenzo the Magnificent and Savonarola, Montaigne and Ignatius Loyola, Marguerite of Navarre and Catherine de' Medici, Calvin and Alexander VI, Benvenuto Cellini and Sir Philip Sidney, Pizarro and Sir Humphrey Gilbert,

Leonardo da Vinci and Browning's Grammarian, the face of Apollo below the crown of thorns, the eyes of Aphrodite under the veil of the Virgin Mother of God—the age is large enough for all these incompatibles to be typical of it. Jusserand[1] draws a vivid picture of the Renaissance spirit, "l'uomo universale," in Elizabeth's own father:

Warrior, statesman, sportsman, physician, musician, theologian, archer, lover, he meddled with all matters and wanted to have every kind of thing in abundance. He would hear, we know, five masses daily, as though heaven were his sole care: he tired ten horses in one chase; he spoke four languages; he appropriated fifteen million sterling of Church property; he wedded six wives; he would have liked to be Emperor and conquer France, to be Pope and well-nigh God in his own land.

Do we wonder if the Elizabethans wrote melodrama when they so lived it? Its stage was hardly wilder than reality, Tamburlaine than Tom Stukely. Not "Nothing too much" but "All to the utmost" is the cry of the time: and Hubris, the Greek vice of 'insolence' is a Renaissance virtue: "turn back, there is no sailing beyond the pillars of Heracles" sings Pindar: and Dante's Ulysses dies for his presumption: but Columbus, like Faust and Tamburlaine steers fearlessly into unknown immensity to find and win. Chapman voices its lust for action.

> Give me a spirit that on life's rough sea
> Loves to have his sails fill'd with a lusty wind
> Even till his ship-yards tremble, his masts crack,
> And his rapt ship runs on her side so low
> That she drinks water and her keel ploughs air.
> There is no danger to a man that knows
> What Life and Death is; there's not any law
> Exceeds his knowledge; neither is it lawful
> That he should stoop to any other law.

[1] *Literary History of the English People*, II, 151.

Marlowe utters its boundless aspiration:

> Our souls whose faculties can comprehend
> The wondrous architecture of the world
> And measure every wandering planet's course,
> Still climbing after knowledge infinite
> Will us to wear ourselves and never rest
> Until we reach the ripest fruit of all.

The Renaissance spirit is indeed like the fabulous bird of Paradise to which Swinburne was once compared, which cannot perch or find rest ever, since Nature has denied it feet.

Jusserand[1] has pointed out how Macbeth and Claudius are only the counterparts of Bothwell. Mary Stuart went in page's clothes, and her rival Elizabeth in her gloomy old age "walks much in her privy chamber and stamps with her feet at ill news and thrusts her rusty sword at times into the arras in great rage" like the slayer of Polonius. The austere Prynne avers that the devil appeared in bodily shape at a performance of *Faustus*. Jonson himself had killed his man, despite a sword "eight inches shorter": and when he was condemned to have nose and ears slit for his share in *Eastward Ho* only his reprieve prevented his old mother poisoning him and herself to escape that shameful punishment.

If the Elizabethan popular stage seems cruel let us remember the heads rotting on London Bridge, or St Bartholomew or the massacre at Smerwick; if it seems savage, let us remember that the gentle Sidney could write to his father's secretary "Mr Molineux, if ever I know you to do so much as read any letter I write to my father without his commandment or my consent I will thrust my dagger into you. And trust to it for I speak in earnest"[2]; or if that stage seems

---

[1] *Literary History of the English People*, III, 294.

[2] Cf. the ingenious Jean de la Taille who says "Tragedy must not deal with things which happen every day, naturally and in accord with reason, such as dying a natural death or being slain by one's enemy."

coarse let us once more remember that Surrey's fair Geraldine used to breakfast off a pound of bacon and a pot of beer and Elizabeth to swear like a fishwife.

Yet this very want of polish, this less veneered, semi-barbarism may have helped to keep out of England the pedantry which elsewhere accompanied the culture of the Renaissance. There might be a general rage of translation in England such that, as Ward[1] points out, Peele could rank with Chaucer and Gower, Phaer the obscure translator of the *Aeneid*, and Elizabeth herself render a chorus of the *Hercules Oetaeus* of Seneca into indifferent English verse; still things like the Greek Academy of Aldus Manutius with its fine for saying anything in any other tongue, and the pontifications of a Cinthio or a Scaliger were kept to the continent.

In brief the Renaissance had rediscovered in the Classics first the worship of earthly and human Beauty for its own sake, whereas Medievalism had typically reserved nudity to the damned in Hell, secondly and still more, the worship of Strength and the Superman. With Nietzsche, its creed was "Was ist gut fragt Ihr? Tapfer sein ist gut." Perhaps that is one more reason why it preferred Rome to Greece, Seneca to Sophocles.

For this preference was no mere chance, and not merely because Latin was more familiar than Greek. The rising infancy of English drama could find nothing in Classics so near its own level as the declining senility of Roman. Nero's Rome had the crudity of surfeit, Elizabethan England the crudity of hunger, his Rome the cruelty of over sophistication and decadence, her England the cruelty of raw and primitive youth. The cruelty and crudity of decadence should be no mystery to us with our gladiatorial press and Mr Kipling for our imperial laureate. It was inevitable that the young England of the Tudors should prefer the "twopence

---

[1] *Eng. Dram. Lit.* I, 189.

coloured" to the "penny plain." The harm was not so great;
Seneca was indeed a poor model; but, as Quintilian observed,
"far better that young writers should err on the side of
exuberance than of jejunity; the one may be pruned, the
other only shrivels more the older it grows." Seneca was near
enough to Renaissance exuberance to appeal to it as a model;
classic enough when taken as a model, to impose upon it a
wholesome sense of structure and of style. And now "blossom
by blossom the spring begins."

CHAPTER V

SENECA IN THE ELIZABETHANS

FROM this point the influence of Seneca becomes more and more diffused and elusive, as, streamlike, it loses itself with other tributaries in the great living ocean of Elizabethan drama. And yet it does maintain itself still very distinctly in one academical succession of minor playwrights which we may deal with first. The Countess of Pembroke, "Sidney's sister, Pembroke's mother" gathered round her a coterie influenced by the French Senecan Garnier (flor. 1563–90). We have here a second wave of Senecan influence in England. She herself translated his *Antonie* in 1590; a little later she succeeded in bringing under her wing, of all wild birds, Kyd whose melodramatic *Spanish Tragedy* of 1585–7 had first really established tragedy on the popular stage. He now produced a version of Garnier's *Cornélie* (c. 1592).

The version is merely a literary curiosity. From the first act to the last nothing whatever happens. Cornelia weeps profusely at the beginning; she weeps even more profusely at the end; other catastrophe there is none. Act I is a five page monologue by Cicero; next the Chorus inveighs against war. Then for eleven pages Cornelia wails, while Cicero consoles her with the Senecan philosophy of life, death and suicide. A reminiscence of the pseudo-Senecan *Octavia* here, a would-be Senecan bout of quip and counterquip there, preserve the due classic colour. Such is Act II. The next Chorus sings of the transience and recurrence of all things. Then in Act III though they might have known better, they in their turn attempt to console the inconsolable heroine. In vain; she has had a most Senecan dream of

> The ghost of Pompey with a ghastly look,
> All pale and brawn-fallen

from which she awoke with the due Senecan shivers—likewise caught from poor Octavia. She leaves the stage. Enter Cicero; three and a half pages of lamentation ensue. Re-enter Cornelia with her servant Philip, who brings Pompey's 'tender bones' in an urn. "O sweet, dear, deplorable cinders" exclaims Cornelia, weeping worse than ever. The Chorus sings of Fortune. Act IV. Cassius and Decimus Brutus discuss the political situation; the Chorus sings of Tyranny. Caesar and Anthony discuss the political situation. A Chorus of Caesar's friends sing of Envy. Act V—a messenger relates for nine pages the defeat and death of Cornelia's father Scipio. Cornelia weeps for four and a half more and the play is happily over. The unities have been religiously observed; not a comic smile has infringed the severe lips of Tragedy; gentility could ask or do no more.

Samuel Daniel's two tragedies in the same style, *Cleopatra* (c. 1593) and *Philotas* (1600-4), are finer stuff. They are brought nearer to their French models by a return from blank verse to rhyme. His *Cleopatra* opens with a nine page monologue by the heroine and ends with a nine page messenger's report of her death. For, as Jusserand points out, Act I Scene 1 of these ultra-classic plays corresponds to Act V Scene 2 in a Shakespearian as far as action is concerned. But though they are not exciting reading, there is a thin clear gracefulness, a reflection of the author's gentle melancholy, throughout.

Philotas is a more vigorous work, dealing with the ruin of that frank and fearless lieutenant of Alexander by his more courtier-like and subtle rivals on a charge of conspiracy against the King.

Both plays are good minor drama. To Seneca through Garnier they owe their form, their philosophising choruses, their line-for-line dialogue. But there is little of the spirit of Seneca the poet, even if Seneca the philosopher is not entirely absent from them. They have none of his crude verse, his unabashed truculence. Daniel writes with a tired hand, content or at least resigned to being little regarded and soon forgotten, the minor poet of a few.

> Years hath done this wrong
> To make me write too much and live too long.

So he sighs in the dedication of *Philotas*, and wearily adds

> as good
> As not to write, as not be understood.

The two oriental Tragedies of Fulke Greville Lord Brooke, friend of Sir Philip Sidney at Shrewsbury and through life, fellow-commoner of Jesus, Cambridge, and councillor of Elizabeth and James, stand by themselves. They are not easy to come at, still less to understand. They are in fact almost dramatic parables of his theories on State and Church, Potentates and Priests. Like his model Seneca Greville himself presents to the puzzled observer a certain contradictoriness. Apparently devout, he yet writes sometimes of 'Providence' in the rebellious tones of Swinburne and Fitzgerald and, with bitter invective against tyranny in both his plays, in public life he yet succeeded in getting himself well enough gilded as a pillar of the throne until finally he was murdered at seventy-four by a servant he had left out of his will. -

The plays first repel, then attract, by their intriguing obscurity. For his style is not only overloaded with meaning and peopled with bevies of Abstractions, till it becomes at times almost like a philosophic Allegory; it also indulges at times in verbal capers which out-Seneca Seneca.

For instance in *Mustapha* Rosten describes his escape from a riot.

I spake; they cried for Mustapha and Achmat.
Some cried " Away," some " Kill," some " Save," some " Hearken."
Those that cried " Save " were those that sought to kill me,
Who cried " Hearke " were those that first brake silence.
They held that bade me goe. Humilitie was guiltie,
Words were reproach, silence in me was scornful.
They answered ere they asked, assured and doubted.
I fled; their furie followed to destroy me;
Fury made haste; haste multiplied their furie;
Each would doe all; none would give place to other.
The hindmost strake; and while the foremost lifted
Their arms to strike, each weapon hindred other.
Their running let their strokes, their strokes their running.
Desire, mortal enemy to desire,
Made them that sought my life, give life unto me.

It is like the skipping of Lebanon, or Sir Thomas Browne's elephant "that hath no joints." Similarly elsewhere Brooke borrows Senecan tags from the *Hippolytus*, *Thyestes*, *Hercules Furens* and other plays.

But as a rule he is not content with reproducing shallow Senecan commonplaces; where the Roman figure-skated he dives. His characters are like sculptures by Mestrovic—hewn as it were out of granite with an intellect of blue steel. His plots have a simplicity, archaic and ferocious, not without grandeur. Senecan situations he imitates repeatedly. In *Alaham* Caelica supports her blind, deposed old father, like Antigone, and refuses to betray his hiding-place in a sepulchral vault, with the same ambiguous protests that "he is among the dead" as Andromache makes to save her little Astyanax in the *Troades*. Again Hala poisons her usurping husband Alaham, as Dejanira Hercules, with a robe, and murders their child before his eyes, as Medea Jason's, and the prologue is spoken by the ghost of one of the old Kings of Ormus. The Choruses of both plays are very various; Priests and Tartars, Time and Eternity, Good Spirits and Ill (rather like Hardy's in *The Dynasts*), discuss with oracular sententiousness the profoundest philosophy. Some of Brooke's obscurity may indeed be intentional—a darkening of the page that made it safer to write between the lines. But at times he is free in speech as in thought and "the lion laughs," for instance, in the Chorus of Priests at the end of *Mustapha* the more readable and less tenebrous of the tragedies.

> Oh wearisome condition of Humanity,
> Borne under one law, to another bound,
> Vainly begot, and yet forbidden vanity,
> Created sick, commanded to be sound.

How it echoes that other cry, where East and West have met once more, in the *Rubaiyat* of Omar—

> O thou that Man of baser earth didst make
> And e'en with Paradise devise the Snake.

There is not time to dwell longer on these forgotten plays. But they are of interest as showing how a profound and highly original mind could accept the Senecan mould, wherein to cast in silence its own strange new alloys of thought. That Fulke Greville, like Montaigne, so honoured him, says almost more for Seneca than Seneca can for himself.

Similar but far simpler and shallower are the four mon-archical Tragedies of William Alexander Earl of Stirling (1603–7). *Croesus*, a dramatisation of the story of Herodotus, *Darius*, on Alexander's conquest of Asia, *The Alexandraean Tragedy*, which deals with the troubles following his death, and, lastly, *Julius Caesar*. They are all extremely Senecan and consumedly dull. To understand why text-books so often mention them by name and never do more than mention them by name, it is only necessary to hunt up and open these happily scarce works[1]. Philosophisings on the blessings of the humble, or feeble rant, of which "Where tigers rage, toads spue, and serpents hiss," is a favourable example, alternate with dismal choruses on the mutability and vanity of all things—queer products for the pen of a Scotsman who feathered his nest extremely well under the first Scottish King of England. It would be hard indeed to find an author who says less or takes longer saying it.

Greville is at least a weird obfuscated genius; Alexander a seedy jackdaw masquerading in mouldy owl's feathers. Such are the chief names in the academic succession of orthodox Classicism from Gorboduc to Stirling.

We must now turn back to the genuine fusion of Academic and Popular, and its typical product the Revenge Tragedy. For at the head of real Elizabethan tragedy stand two epoch-making plays, which at once became in some measure themselves classics. *The Spanish Tragedy* and *Tamburlaine* are the types respectively of what may be called the Revenge-play and the Conqueror-play. The former is both the more important and the more Senecan.

Kyd's *Spanish Tragedy* was performed about 1586—laughed at by the few, doted on by the many both in England and abroad. It opens with the ghost of Andrea, slain in battle with the Portuguese, and the Spirit of Revenge; these two perform the part of the Senecan chorus throughout the play. Bell' Imperia, niece of the King of Spain had been Andrea's mistress. She now falls in love with Horatio, son of Hieronimo, marshal of Spain, the young warrior who had revenged Andrea by capturing his slayer Balthazar, son of the Viceroy of Portingal. But Bell' Imperia's brother Lorenzo is bent on wedding her to this same Balthazar: the two men surprise Horatio with her and hang him. His old father finds him

---

[1] Recently a new edition has been published by Kastner and Charlton (Manchester University Press).

murdered and learns from Bell' Imperia and other sources, who are the murderers. Bell' Imperia's marriage with Balthazar is now celebrated. Hieronimo arranges with her that they shall enact before the King and Viceroy a marriage play in which she stabs, but in deadly earnest, Balthazar, then herself, while Hieronimo similarly kills Lorenzo, reveals the truth to his horrified royal audience, bites out his tongue and stabs himself in turn.

Very melodramatic, but apart from its chorus and two Latin quotations from Seneca's *Tragedies*, and apart from its revenge motif and its plethora of allusions to

> Minos, Aeacus, and Rhadamant

Ixion, Tityus, Sisyphus and the rest of infernal society, it does not retain a great deal that is definitely Senecan. It is already rather flesh and blood, than merely blood and thunder.

Much more Senecan is a far less important production of about the same year, the worthless *Locrine* attributed once to Shakespeare, now to Peele.

The Chorus is supplied by Ate in black who brings in a different dumb show at the beginning of each Act, viz. a lion and a bear, Perseus and Andromeda, a crocodile and a snake, Omphale and Hercules, and Jason and Medea; she also provides the epilogue. The tragic characters rant in Cambises' vein; the comic enact more than usually idiotic buffoonery. The ghost of Albanact appears thrice, that of Corineus once, both squeaking for Revenge:

> The boisterous Boreas thundreth forth Revenge,
> The stony rocks cry out on sharp revenge,
> The thorny bush pronounceth dire revenge,
> Now Corineus stay and see revenge.

There is the usual chatter of

> Tantal's hunger and Ixion's wheel,

of Tartarus and Puryflegethon. There is also a passage of very Senecan stichomuthia. In fact the whole play well answers the oft quoted gibes of the *Warning for Fair Women* (1599) at the stock absurdities of contemporary Senecan tragedy.

> How some damned tyrant to obtain a crown
> Stabs, hangs, imprisons, smothers, cutteth throats
> And then a chorus too comes howling in
> And tells us of the worrying of a cat:
> Then too a filthy whining ghost
> Lapt in some foul sheet or a leather pilch
> Comes screaming like a pig half stick'd
> And cries "Vindicta"—Revenge, revenge.

However in spite of the *Warning*, the Revenge play after its first success in the *Spanish Tragedy* was long to continue both popular and Senecan. The lost original *Hamlet*, probably by Kyd (1587), his *Soliman and Persida* (1588), *Titus Andronicus* (1585–90), *Lust's Dominion* (1590), *The True Tragedie of Richard III* (1591) and Shakespeare's *Richard III* (1593), Marston's *Antonio and Mellida* (1599), Chettle's *Hoffmann* (1602), Shakespeare's *Hamlet* (1602), the four main plays of Tourneur and Webster, Chapman's *Revenge of Bussy d'Ambois* (1604), *Macbeth* (1605–6), Beaumont and Fletcher's *Triumph of Death* (1608) all belong to this particular genre, and most of them, especially Marston and Chapman, show definite Senecan influence.

Kyd's *Soliman and Persida*, a far weaker play than the *Spanish Tragedy*, tries to make up for it by wholesale slaughter. The Chorus is supplied by Fortune, Love and Death, who dispute pre-eminence; as there are no less than eighteen murders in the piece, and only 'supers' survive to carry out the corpses, Death is an easy victor.

Titus Andronicus, which Shakespeare probably at least worked over, and which yielded in popularity only to the *Spanish Tragedy*, is more Senecan than ever.

Cunliffe points out that the fine passage I, 1, ll. 150–156:

In peace and honour rest you here my sons.
Rome's readiest champions, repose you here in rest
Secure from worldly chances and mishaps!
Here lurks no treason, here no envy swells,
Here grow no damned drugs, here are no storms
No noise, but silence, and eternal sleep;
In peace and honour rest you here my sons!

is modelled on *Troades* 145–161.

"Felix Priamus," dicite cunctae,
liber manes vadit ad imos

.   .   .   .   .   .

nunc Elysii nemoris tutus
errat in umbris
interque pias felix animas
Hectora quaerit. Felix Priamus!

There are also two garbled Latin quotations from Seneca's tragedies. The valley where Bassianus is murdered (II, 3) is not unlike the scene of Atreus' slaughter of Thyestes' sons (*Thyest.* 651–82) and Cunliffe[1] also quotes other passages, which it must be owned, really indicate nothing. Only too many of these literary parallels are like the geometrical sort, in that though followed back to infinity, they never meet. As Gibbon remarked, if I remember, of a Shakespearian parallel with St Gregory Nazianzen, "Shakespeare had never read St Gregory; but the language of nature is the same in England and in Cappadocia."

Quite unquestionable however is the Senecan indebtedness of the last scene, where Tamora is treated to a Thyestean pie in which her own son's flesh is baked, and four murders are perpetrated in the brevity of twenty lines.

Again *The True Tragedie of Richard III* (1591), which appears to owe something to Legge's play mentioned above, is chiefly of interest because Shakespeare used it. It is a

---

[1] *Influence of Seneca on Elizabethan Tragedy*, pp. 71–72.

wooden piece with definite Senecan traces, such as an opening
scene with Clarence's ghost gibbering,

> Cresce cruor, sanguis satietur sanguine, cresce.
> Quod spero, sitio. Sitio, sitio vindictam,

not very good hexameters even for a royal ghost; then enter
Truth and Poetrie as a sort of chorus to make a brief dis-
quisition.

The most notable and poetic passage by far is Richard's
soliloquy before Bosworth when the author does stagger out
of his jog-trot into a gallop of sorts. It may give some notion
of the extreme revengefulness of revenge tragedy.

> Meethinkes their ghoasts come gaping for revenge
> Whom I have slain in reaching for a crowne.
> Clarence complains and crieth for revenge,
> My Nephues bloods, "Revenge, revenge" doth crie.
> The headlesse Peers come pressing for revenge,
> And everyone cries, "let the tyrant die."
> The Sunne by day shines hotely for revenge,
> The Stars are turned to Comets for revenge,
> The Planets change their courses for revenge,
> The birds sing not, but sorrow for revenge,
> The silly lambe sits bleating for revenge,
> The screeking Raven sits croking for revenge,
> Whole heads of beasts come bellowing for revenge,
> And all, yea all the world I think
> Cries for revenge and nothing but revenge.

Shakespeare's *Richard III* (1593) has been called his nearest
approach to Aeschylus; not very convincingly. Is it as near
for instance as *Macbeth*? But it is certainly (not counting
Titus Andronicus) his nearest to Seneca; and his next nearest
to Seneca is once more—*Macbeth*. Yet the nearness is at
closest somewhat remote.

Richard is indeed a typical Senecan tyrant; the ghosts
which haunt Clarence's last night and still more those which
haunt Richard's, the half-choric part played by the wild old

queen Margaret as embodiment of the curse of the House of
Plantagenet, are all frankly based on Senecan practice.

Again the long passages of epigrammatic Stichomuthia are
specially typical.

Anne.   No beast so fierce but knows some touch of pity.
Gloucester. But I know none and therefore am no beast.
A.   Oh wonderful when devils tell the truth!
Gl. Oh wonderful when angels are so angry!   (Act I, Sc. 2.)

(Richard demands Elizabeth's daughter as his bride.)

King Richard. Say she shall be a high and mighty queen.
Q. El.   To wail the title as her mother doth.
K. Rich. Say I will love her everlastingly.
Q. El.   But how long shall that title "ever" last?
K. Rich. Sweetly in force until her fair life's end.
Q. El.   But how long fairly shall her sweet life last?
K. Rich. As long as heaven and nature lengthens it.
Q. El.   As long as hell and Richard likes of it.
K. Rich. Your reasons are too shallow and too quick.
Q. El.   O, no my reasons are too deep and dead,
           Too deep and dead, poor infants, in their graves.
K. Rich. Harp not on that string, madam, that is past.
Q. El.   Harp on it still shall I till heart strings break.
K. Rich. Now by my George, my garter, and my crown,—
Q. El.   Profan'd, dishonoured, and the third usurped.
K. Rich. I swear—
Q. El.   By nothing for that is no oath.
K. Rich. Now by the world,—
Q. El.   'Tis full of thy foul wrongs.
K. Rich. My father's death,—
Q. El.   Thy life hath that dishonour'd.
K. Rich. Then by myself,—
Q. El.   Thy self is self-misus'd.
K. Rich. Why then, by God,—
Q. El.   God's wrong is most of all.
           If thou hadst fear'd to break an oath by him,
           The unity the King my husband made,
           Had not been broken nor my brothers died.
                                        (Act IV, Sc. 4.)

These altercations in a classical regularity unusual for
Shakespeare, have all Seneca's cleverness with none of his
tinsel inhumanity. The industry of Cunliffe and J. Engel[1] has
also discovered several of the usual sort of parallel passages,
for instance the comparison of evil presentiment to a ground-
swell at sea.

> By a divine instinct men's minds mistrust
> Ensuing dangers: as by proof we see
> The waters swell before a boisterous storm.
>
> (*Rich. III*, 11, 3.)
>
> Mittit luctus signa futuri
> Mens ante sui praesaga mali.
> Instat nautis fera tempestas
> Cum sine vento tranquilla tument.
>
> "Man's mind can presage ills to be
> By bodings dark of destiny,
> As tempests threat the mariner's sail,
> When calm seas swell without a gale."
>
> (*Thyestes* 957–61.)

Similarly in *Macbeth* besides the general resemblance of
the atmosphere of murder, of the supernatural, and revenge
there is the famous parallel already noticed by Lessing (1784).
In the *Hercules Furens*, the hero awakes to find he has
murdered his wife and children.

> Quis Tanais aut quis Nilus aut quis Persica
> Violentus unda Tigris aut Rhenus ferox
> Tagusve Hibera turbidus gaza fluens
> Abluere dextram poterit? arctoum licet
> Maeotis in me gelida transfundat mare
> Et tota Tethys per meas currat manus,
> Haerebit altum facinus.[2]   (Cf. *Phaedra* 715–7.)

---

[1] *Preussisches Jahrbuch*, April, 1903.
[2] Translated above, p. 77.

So Macbeth cries:

> What hands are here! Ha! They pluck out mine eyes[1]?
> Will all great Neptune's ocean wash this blood
> Clean from my hand? No this my hand will rather
> The multitudinous seas incarnadine
> Making the green, one red,   (II, 2.)

and Lady Macbeth, "All the perfumes of Arabia will not sweeten this little hand."

There are other more doubtful similarities. Lady Macbeth's invocation of the spirits of Murder (I, 5, 40–53), may owe something to Medea's (*Medea* 1–25), and the cry heard by Macbeth (II, 2, 37–41):

> Macbeth doth murder sleep, the innocent sleep,
> Sleep that links up the ravell'd sleeve of care,
> The death of each day's life, sore labour's bath,
> Balm of hurt minds, great nature's second course,
> Chief nourisher in life's feast—

may have been in some slight way suggested by another adjoining passage of the *Hercules*, the Chorus after the mad hero has slain his dearest:

> Tuque o domitor, Somne, malorum,
> Requies animi.   (*Hercules Furens* 1066–81.)
> "Thou O sleep that calmest ill,
> Rest of man's soul..."

though I confess to seeing but little resemblance. Once more "Canst thou not minister to a mind diseased?" (V, 3, 40) has been paired with:

> No man can heal
> A mind polluted; death must medicine crime.
> (*Hercules Furens* 1261.)

But it must be said once for all about the bulk of Shakespeare's supposed borrowings from Seneca, that one grows more and more sceptical; with Chapman and Marston, as we shall see, the evidence of actual indebtedness is convincing.

---

[1] Is he thinking of Oedipus too? The original Sophoclean passage (*v.* p. 77 above) occurs *in* the Messenger's account of his self-blinding.

But most of the Shakespearian passages quoted by Cunliffe and Engel seems to me the merest coincidences. For instance because in 2 *Henry VI*, I, 4, a spirit is conjured up, because in 2 and 3 *Henry VI* there is much bloodshed and some fatalism, we are asked to believe that their author, whether Shakespeare or another, is there too showing Senecan influence[1]. But though Seneca loved ghosts and penny-dreadfulness, he had no monopoly in that. Senecan ghosts and Senecan horrors conform always to a certain wide but definite type; the spirit in *Henry VI* has nothing specifically Senecan about him: and to cry 'Seneca' every time the lights burn blue is preposterous. As well argue from the witch of Endor and Samuel's ghost, that Seneca inspired the author of that part of Holy Writ.

Of *Hamlet* indeed one may say that the ghost is of the true Senecan type (cf. Tantalus in the *Thyestes*, Laius in the *Oedipus*), but that type was so naturalised in England by this time that Shakespeare had no need to import him all the way from Rome.

In short though Shakespeare almost certainly had read Seneca, though he may even have read him in the original, and though he seems here and there to echo him, the number and importance of such echoes seem to have been very much exaggerated.

Of all the popular Elizabethans Seneca's greatest debtor is Marston, especially in the Two Parts of *Antonio and Mellida*. In these there are no less than nine Latin quotations from the plays of Seneca, one of them eight lines long, besides a long passage from his prose *De Providentia*: there are as well other tags Englished in the normal Elizabethan way, such as:

> Well ere your sun set, I'll show myself myself
> Worthy my blood. I was a Duke: that's all.
> No matter whither but from whence we fall.
>
> (Pt I, Act III, Sc. 1; cf. *Thyestes* 926.)

---

[1] Cunliffe, *Influence of Seneca on Elizabethan Tragedy*, pp. 72–73.

The Senecan morbidity strengthens towards the close; Antonio in revenge for his father, Andrugio, murders his sister's little son by, the villain, Piero, Duke of Venice, in a scene of laboured eeriness, midnight in St Mark's Church, with two of the usual ghosts groaning 'Murder!' from the vaults beneath; and in the final scene, Piero's tongue is torn out and he is presented with his little son's limbs in a dish, with the sneer of Atreus in the *Thyestes*:

> Thy son? true: and which is my most joy
> I hope no bastard, but thy very blood,
> Thy true-begotten, most legitimate
> And loved issue—there's the comfort on it.

Having tortured and stabbed him the conspirators take the edifying resolution thenceforth to

> live enclosed
> In holy verge of some religious order,
> Most constant votaries,   (Pt II, Act v, 2.)

and the curtain falls.

It is a perpetual riddle how audiences could stomach these same old fetid horrors, these banquets of human flesh, staler and staler every time.

Far happier is the reminiscence of the famous "Medea superest" (*Medea* 166) in the speech of the broken and defeated Andrugio, Duke of Genoa:

> Triumphs not Venice in my overthrow?
> Gapes not my native country for my blood?
> Lies not my son tomb'd in the swelling main?
> And yet more lowering fate! There's nothing left
> Unto Andrugio but Andrugio.
> And that nor mischief, force, distress nor hell can take;
> Fortune my fortunes, not my mind, shall shake.
>   (Pt I, Act III, Sc. I.)

If however Marston paid Seneca so constantly the truest form of flattery, he stood well this side idolatry. In the

Malcontent, which shows clear though fewer Senecan traces, when Bilioso, who boasts some acquaintance with the outsides of books, begins "Marry I remember one Seneca, Lucius Annaeus Seneca"—Piero breaks in, "Out upon him! he writ of temperance and fortitude, yet lived like a voluptuous epicure, and died like an effeminate coward"—a diatribe so manifestly untrue of Seneca's death that the Duke may have been confounding him with his nephew Lucan.

Truer rings Antonio's denunciation. Antonio, his father dead and his love shamed, seeks consolation in the *De Providentia* (VI, 4), but after four glib lines on the contempt of pain and grief, breaks out:

> Pish, thy mother was not lately widowed,
> Thy dear affied love lately defam'd
> With blemish of foul lust, when thou wrot'st thus.
> Thou wrapt in furs, beaking thy limbs fore fires,
> Forbidst the frozen zone to shudder. Ha! 'tis nought
> But foamy bubbling of a fleamy brain,
> Nought else but smoke.

We cannot follow the slighter borrowings and shadowings of the *Malcontent*, the *Fawn*, and *Sophonisba*[1]. Once Marston's method is clear, exhaustive details of his practice can add little. If he owes Seneca some of his worst crudities, he owes him too some of his finest speeches in the purple vein of Renaissance individualism.—We read to-day these stale Senecan horrors, as we view old, dark stains of blood in some historic room, with too strong a feeling of remoteness and unreality to be nauseated. But his Senecan defiances of doom, brave words of broken men, can wake some living echoes still.

Chapman's contribution to this type of play is the *Revenge of Bussy d'Ambois*. But in this same connexion we may deal with the three kindred dramas, *Bussy d'Ambois*, and the two

---

[1] *Vide* Cunliffe, *Influence of Seneca on Elizabethan Tragedy*, pp. 98–107.

tragedies of Byron, all works which betray the reader of
Seneca as well as the translator of Homer.

Thus Act II of *Bussy* introduces a most pompous and
circumstantial Nuntius of the great duel between him and
Barrisor.

> What Atlas or Olympus lifts his head
> So far past covert, that with air enough
> My words may be informed and from his height
> I may be seen and heard through all the world?
> A tale so worthy and so fraught with wonder
> Sticks in my jaws and labours with event.

There is a passage of equally Senecan stichomuthia on the
Senecan commonplace of birth and worth. D'Ambois has
just been engaged in taunt and counter-taunt with Guise in
the presence of Henry of Valois.

> *Montsurry.* Peace, peace I pray thee, peace.
> *Bussy.* Let him peace first
>   That made the first war.
> *Mont.* He's the better man.
> *Bussy.* And therefore may do worst?
> *Mont.* He has more titles.
> *Bussy.* So Hydra has more heads.
> *Mont.* He's greater known.
> *Bussy.* His greatness is the people's: mine's mine own.
> *Mont.* He's nobly born.
> *Bussy.* He is not, I am, noble.   (III, 1.)

There is too a more generous than happy use of the supernatural in the two D'Ambois plays. In the first the Friar,
who panders to Bussy, raises Behemoth with a Latin incan-
tation and being shortly after slain appears under the strange
hybrid title "Umbra Friar," and having appeared, seems to
find it as impossible to disappear as a nervous guest at a
tea-party. A peculiar trait of Chapman's ghosts is that his
living characters are seldom more than mildly interested in
their apparition. In the *Revenge*, after Clermont has killed

Montsurry comes the direction—"Music and the ghost of
Bussy enters, leading the Ghosts of the Guise, Monsieur,
Cardinal Guise and Chatillon: they dance about the dead
body and Exeunt." Clermont is indeed surprised, but only
because he had supposed the Guise and the Cardinal were
still living. Had they been dead, nothing presumably could
have been more ordinary than this ghostly gavotte (v, 1).

Earlier in the same Act with an obvious reminiscence of
the Shade of Agrippina in the *Octavia*, Umbra Bussy rises
to claim vengeance.

> Up from the Chaos of eternal night
> (To which the whole digestion of the world
> Is now returning) once more I ascend
> And bide the cold damp of this piercing air.

But as usual in Chapman, though he borrows Senecan
mannerisms, his matter is his own.

His heroes again, have all the Senecan egotism, and in the
Revenge, Clermont D'Ambois, the dead Bussy's brother and
avenger declaims it by the page; in Act v he states the Stoic
creed of resignation to the "high and general Cause," to
"great Necessity," like a very Chrysippus.

> A man to join himself with th' Universe
> In his man's way and make (in all things fit)
> One with the All, and go on, round as it:
> Not plucking from the whole his wretched part
> And into straits or into nought revert,
> Wishing the complete Universe might be
> Subject to such a rag of it as he.

It takes an army to arrest him; and even they cannot stop
his philosophic preachments.

> In short, this Senecal man is found in him
> He may with heaven's immortal powers compare,
> To whom the day and fortune equal are:
> Come fair or foul, whatever chance can fall,
> Fix'd in himself, he still is one to all.   (iv. 1.)

There are also several clear adaptations of Seneca in the two Byron plays.

Thus the passage where La Brosse the astrologer begs Byron not to make him disclose the result of his divinations (*Conspiracy of Byron*, III, 1), is clearly modelled on Creon's similar request to Oedipus, after Tiresias has questioned the ghost of Laius (*Oed.* 511–29).

Similarly in V, 1, the line

Byron. What can he do? *D'Auvergne.* All that you cannot fear,

is probably based on *Agamemnon* 799:

Agam. What can the victor fear? *Cassandra.* What he fears not.

There are also in Act V, 1, of both the *Conspiracy* and of the *Tragedy of Byron* echoes of that trick remark of the *Hercules Furens*, "I have lost all my blessings even my madness."

These resemblances are often trivial: they are given with exhaustive care in Cunliffe's monograph[1], and there is no need to multiply them. At least in Chapman and Marston, the deeper one goes, the more convincing the indebtedness does become.

It was indeed of Chapman's play that Dryden wrote "A famous modern poet used to sacrifice every year a Statius to Virgil's Manes and I have indignation enough to burn a *D'Ambois* annually to the memory of Jonson." A little hard; although Chapman might have written better without Seneca's influence, for he was himself only too sententiously prolix by nature. Well indeed had he followed rather Homer, the master poet whom he so happily rendered into English verse, and whose inspiration subtly breathes in the sombre majesty of the dying words of Charles, Duke of Byron.

[1] *The Influence of Seneca on Elizabethan Tragedy.*

Such is the endless exile of dead men.
Summer succeeds the spring; autumn the summer;
The frosts of winter the fall'n leaves of autumn.
All these, and all fruits in them yearly fade
And every year return; but cursèd man
Shall never more resume his vanished face.
                              (*Tragedy of Byron* v, 1.)

The traces in Tourneur and Webster are far fainter. The first-named quotes in the *Revenger's Tragedy*, 1, 4, the hackneyed

Curae leves loquuntur, ingentes stupent,
                              (*Phaedra* 607.)

and a Stoic commonplace is the thread of Charlemont's defiance in the *Atheist's Tragedy*.

I was a baron. That thy father has
Deprived me of. Instead of that I am
Created king. I've lost a signiory
That was confined within a piece of earth,
A wart upon the body of the world.
But now I am the emperor of a world,
This little world of man. My passions are
My subjects and I can command them laugh,
Whilst thou dost tickle them to death with misery.

But Stoicism by this was become almost as much Elizabethan as Senecan; and the same applies to the bloodshed and vices, ghosts and skulls of Webster and Tourneur. In them the Revenge-play has culminated; after them it fades.

The Conqueror-plays, *Tamburlaine*, *The Battle of Alcazar*, *Selimus* and the rest concern us less. Though the rant of the Scythian is in the vein of Hercules at his maddest, Marlowe's play shows little specifically Senecan, less indeed than Peele's imitation *Alcazar* with its Precentor doing duty for a Chorus, its infernal catalogue of Ixion and the rest, and its "Enter three ghosts crying Vindicta"; less too than Greene's *Selimus*, with its description of the *Golden Age* (240–50) based on the *Phaedra*, its scepticism recalling the *Troades*, its long dialogue on kingship practically translated from *Thyestes*,

> It is the greatest glorie of a king
> When tho' his subjects hate his wicked deeds
> Yet are they forst to bear them all with praise. (1314–16.)

Typical of contemporary taste is the epilogue.

> If this first part, Gentles, do like you well,
> The second part shall greater murders tell.

There remains one great figure, even more classical, though less specifically Senecan than the school of Pembroke and Daniel—Ben Jonson.

The same dogmas of tyranny just quoted are echoed in *Sejanus*, II, 2.

> where
> The subject is no less compell'd to bear
> Than praise his sovereign's acts.

The speech in the same scene:

> Adultery! it is the lightest ill
> I will commit. A race of wicked acts
> Shall flow out of my anger and o'erspread
> The world's wide face which no posterity
> Shall e'er approve nor yet keep silent; things
> That for their cunning, close and cruel mark
> Thy father would wish his,

may be taken as an instance of the closeness of such borrowing. For a literal translation of Atreus' corresponding words (*Thyestes*, 46–7, 192–5) runs

> Then be adultery the lightest crime
> In this foul house...Come dare, my soul, a deed
> Such as posterity shall ne'er forget,
> But ne'er keep silent. Some crime must be dared
> Bloody and cruel, a crime such as my brother
> Would wish for his.

In *Catiline* and the fragmentary *Fall of Mortimer* there is also a Senecan chorus; in *Catiline* the ghost of Sylla speaks the usual Senecan ghost's prologue; and, not to dwell on other Senecan loans, even that abused passage of the *Hercules Furens*

> si novi Herculem
> Lycus Creonti debitas poenas dabit.
> Lentum est "dabit": dat: hoc quoque est lentum—dedit.
> (642-4.)

is adapted into

> "He shall die,—
> 'Shall' was too slowly said; he's dying; that
> Is yet too slow; he's dead."   (*Cat.* III, 5.)

Similarly the feeble crudities of Hippolytus' rending piece-meal in the *Phaedra* are reproduced in the fate of Sejanus. The fragmentary Hippolytus is in Theseus' ludicrous phrase "saepe efferendus," "needing many burials"; likewise Sejanus

> So lies he nowhere and yet often buried.   (v, 10.)

It would be possible to follow the Senecan trail further into the flowery meads of Beaumont and Fletcher, the dignity of Massinger or the quieter gloom of Ford. But it grows too faint and derivative until at last it fails altogether in the first twilight of the English stage, and the mutterings of the coming Civil War.

But perhaps the most striking evidence of the pervasive imitation of Seneca, whether at first or second or third hand, may be found by tracing the reappearance of some of his most quoted lines in playwright after playwright. For instance the one line

> Per scelera semper sceleribus tutum est iter.
> "The only path that's safe for crime is crime,"
> (*Agam.* 115.)

is, as Cunliffe shows, quoted in Latin in the *Spanish*

Tragedy and Marston's *Malcontent,* and more or less freely paraphrased in *Misfortunes of Arthur, Macbeth, Richard III, Catiline, The White Devil* and Massinger's *Duke of Milan.*

Curae leves loquuntur, ingentes stupent,

" 'Tis little griefs that speak, great ones are dumb,"

(*Phaedra* 607.)

is reproduced in the play of *Sir Thomas More* and in Tourneur's *Revenger's Tragedy,* paraphrased in *Macbeth* and expanded in Ford's *Broken Heart.*

It was no secret at the time; well known are the gibes of Nash in his preface to Greene's *Menaphon* (1589), about those "vain-glorious tragedians" that feed on nought but "crummes that fall from the translator's trencher." "English Seneca read by candlelight" he sneers "yieldes manie good sentences—'Bloud is a begger' and so forth; and if you intreate him faire in a frostie morning, he will afford you whole Hamlets, I should say handfulls, of tragical speeches." But, he adds, this plagiarists' quarry cannot last always. "Seneca, let blood, line by line and page by page, at length must needes die to our stage."

But after all it is not as a source of petty plagiarisms, as an ancient ruin turned into a Renaissance quarry, that Seneca has mattered. From him men once learned, as well as stole; in him they found again, as the world awoke from its long sleep, the Classic sense of form and structure, of Unity, the true as well as the false; in him the tragic splendour of Human Will in the face of eyeless Destiny, the tragic terror of wild passion, the terror of madness, the terror of the world beyond the grave—something of the grace, the greatness, and the sadness of the Greek, something of that divine fire still quickening the Roman clay.

His work is little remembered, still less regarded now; the ill he wrote has been buried long ago. But the good in his influence was to prove happier and longer-lived. That his greatness was so largely thrust upon him by circumstance, is not a reason for ignoring it. He will never again be the colossus who bestrode the imagination of Scaliger and Sidney; yet it is only fair that the virtue of his literary posterity should be a little visited on the ancestor of Chapman and Marston, Ben Jonson and Shakespeare, Alfieri and Racine. If you seek his memorial, look round on the Tragic stage of England, France and Italy.

INDEX

Accius, 10, 22–24
Adam, 83
Aeschylus, 6, 8, 9, 14
Agamemnon (of Seneca), see Seneca
Agrippina, 35–8, 40
Alabaster, see *Roxana*
Alexander, W., 114–5
Andronicus, L., 15, 19
Annaeus Mela, 26–8
Annaeus Novatus (Gallio), 26–7, 41
Attalus, 28–9

Bale, J., 89–90
Brittanicus, 36–8
Brooke, Lord, see Greville
Buchanan, 95
Burrus, 36–8, 40–1

Chapman, 106, 117, 125–9
Chorus, 5, 7–8, 10–11, 13, 72, 74–6, 94–5, 96, 101–2, 110–7, 129, 131
Church, see Liturgic Drama
Cinthio, 94–5
Classicism, 1–5, 53, 59, 61, 65, 103–4, 132
Claudius, 30, 36–7

Damon and Pithias, 90
Daniel, S , *Cleopatra*, 111–2; *Philotas*, 111–2
Dolce, 95

Ecerinis, 92–3
Ennius, 10, 20–2, 60
Euripides, 3, 8, 9, 11–4

Feast of Fools, 81–2
Filostrato e Panfila, 94
Folk Dramas, 6–8, 81
Ford, 131–2

Gager, 97–9
Gallio, see Annaeus
Garnier, 95
Ghost, 11, 94–5, 97, 99, 102, 111, 113, 115–7, 118–9, 123–4, 126–7, 129, 131

Gismond of Salerne, 94–101
Gorboduc, 5, 96
Greene, 129–30, 132
Greville, Fulke, *Alaham*, 112–3; *Mustapha*, 113–4

Harrowing of Hell, 81
Helvia, 26
Heywood, Jasper, 78, 100
Hrotsvitha, 91

Interludes, 90, 103

Jocasta, 101
Jongleurs, 79–80
Jonson, Ben, *Catiline*, 104, 131–2; *Sejanus*, 130
Julia, 30–1

Kyd, *Cornelia*, 110–1 , *Hamlet*, 117; *Soliman and Persida*, 117–8; *Spanish Tragedy*, 100, 103, 115–6, 131

Legge, 97
Liturgic Drama, 82–3, 88–9
Locrine, 116–7
Lucan, 26, 28

Mankind, 89, 107
Marlowe, 20–1, 103, 115, 129
Marston, 117, 123–5, 132
Massinger, 131–2
Mela, see Annaeus
Messalina, 31, 33–5
Mimi, 24, 79–81
Minstrels, 79–81
Misfortunes of Arthur, 102–3, 132
Moralities, 89
Mundus et Infans, 89
Mussato, 92
Mysteries, 83

Naevius, 19
Nero, 35 *sqq.*
Novatus, see Annaeus

Orbecche, 94–5

Pacuvius, 10, 22
Pembroke, Countess of, 110
Piso, Conspiracy of, 42–4
Poppaea, 40, 41, 44

Recitations, Public, 56
Renaissance, 53–4, 104–9
Richard III, The True Tragedie of, 117–9
Roman Tragedy, of the Republic, 14–24, after Seneca, 78–9
Romanticism, 2–5, 88, 103–4
Roxana, 58, 99

Sacrament, Play of the, 85
Scaliger, 78
Seneca the Elder, 26–7
Seneca the Younger, *Agamemnon,* 61, 66, 67, 69, 70, 131; *Hercules Furens*, 57, 61, 64, 67–8, 70, 75–7, 121–2; *Hercules Oetaeus*, 61, 131; *Medea*, 61, 67–8, 74–5, 77, 122; *Octavia*, 60, 127; *Oedipus*, 61, 63, 64, 70, 128; *Phaedra*, 57, 61, 66, 70–1, 77, 131; *Phoenissae*, 61, 64, 69, 70; *Thyestes*, 61–2, 64, 67, 70, 94, 97, 118, 121, 130; *Troades*, 61,

Seneca the Younger, *Troades (contd)* 64, 65–6, 67, 70, 72, 74, 76, 97, 118
Shakespeare, *Hamlet*, 117, 123, 132; *Henry VI*, 123; *Macbeth*, 117, 121–2, 132; *Richard III*, 97, 117, 119–21, 132; *Titus Andronicus*, 117–8
Siriz, Dame, 80
Sofonisba (of Trissino), 94
Sophocles, 8, 9, 14, 18
Spanish Tragedy, see Kyd
Stirling, Earl of, see Alexander
Stoicism, 13, 22, 47–52, 56, 59, 60, 71, 127–9

Thespis, 6–8, 89
Tourneur, 117, 129, 132
Townley Shepherds' Play, 86–8
"Tragedy," meaning of, 91–2
Trissino, 94

University Latin Plays, 95 *sqq.*

Villains, 11

Warning for Fair Women, 117
Webster, 117, 132
Wyt and Science, Marriage of, 89

PRINTED IN ENGLAND BY J. B PEACE, M A
AT THE CAMBRIDGE UNIVERSITY PRESS

Lightning Source UK Ltd.
Milton Keynes UK
UKHW020705250722
406332UK00006B/673

9 781375 882422